Longman Handbooks for Language Teachers

Nick Dawson

KV-679-255

Teaching on Holiday Courses

Consultant editor: Janet McAlpin

London and New York

Longman Group UK Limited
Longman House, Burnt Mill, Harlow
Essex CM 20 2JE, UK
and associated companies throughout the world.

Distributed in the United States of America
by Longman Publishing, New York

© Longman Group UK Ltd 1990

First published 1990
Second impression 1991

British Library Cataloging in Publication Data
Dawson, Nick
  Teaching on holiday courses.
  1. Vacation courses
  I. title II. McAlpin, Janet
  370

  ISBN 0 582 06463 5

Set in 10/12pt Times

Produced by Longman Singapore Publishers Pte Ltd
Printed in Singapore

Library of Congress Cataloging in Publication Data
Dawson, Nick
  Teaching on holiday courses / Nick Dawson.
      p.   cm. -- (Longman handbooks for
language teachers)
  ISBN 0 582 06463 5
  1. Vacation schools--Great Britain--Handbooks,
  manuals, etc.
  2. Language and languages--Study and teaching--
  Great Britain--Handbooks, manuals, etc. 3. Activity
  programs in education--Great Britain--Handbooks,
  manuals, etc. 4. Students--Travel--Great Britain--
  Handbooks, manuals, etc. I. Title. II. Series.
  LC5756.G8D39   1990
  374′.8′0941--dc20   89-48208
                                                  CIP

AUTHOR'S ACKNOWLEDGEMENTS

This book is the result of many years' experience in the field of holiday language courses. Like many EFL teachers, my entry into the profession was through work on a holiday language course in 1969. Since that time I have worked on several courses for various organisations. No book which is based on experience can be credited to the single individual who tapped the computer keyboard so I would like to acknowledge the influence of many colleagues and friends.

I would like to thank Dr R. O. Friedrich, the President of European School Service, who, for the past ten years has employed me as a language school consultant. Through my work for ESS, I have visited nearly a hundred schools around Britain. In all the schools I have been received with courtesy and hospitality. I have observed lessons and talked with teachers and students. I have been shown the sports, social and excursion programmes and seen the work of accommodation and welfare staff. The directors of the schools have openly and candidly discussed their administrative difficulties. I owe a tremendous debt to the directors and staff of these many schools.

I would also like to thank Mark Berridge for his invaluable contributions to the section on sporting activities, Gaetano Caterino, for his insights on the work of group leaders and my sister Patricia for comments on the role and feelings of a host family.

Finally, I would particularly like to thank Janet McAlpin who has commented on the various stages of growth of this book and has made most helpful suggestions. Her wisdom, sensitivity and knowledge of holiday course teaching has been enormously valuable.

Photograph on page 88–89 by Longman Photo Unit,
John Birdsall Photography and Rosi Jillett.

Contents

A NOTE TO THE READER

A successful holiday language course is the result of the combined efforts of all the members of staff working as a team. The members will each have their own special areas of responsibility but they need to understand the work of their colleagues if they are to function effectively.

You will see from the contents page that this book divides the different areas of responsibility much as they would be divided in a school staff. Each chapter or section is addressed to the specialists in that area but are useful to all the staff.

A holiday language course brings together, for a brief period of intensive activity, staff members who are usually strangers to each other. It is not easy to develop an efficient team in so short a time often because each staff member has little knowledge or understanding of the aims and responsibilities of their colleagues. I hope that this book will give you some of that knowledge and understanding.

This book refers primarily to courses in Britain but many other countries offer holiday language courses. In the English speaking world, I know that Malta, Ireland, Australia and the USA have established centres and of course there have been holiday language centres for French and German as foreign languages for many years.

It strikes me that the principles for a successful holiday language course do not change wherever the course is situated and whatever the language being studied, so I hope that this book will also be of value outside Britain.

BRITISH COUNCIL RECOGNITION AND ARELS-FELCO

Schools in Britain which are members of ARELS-FELCO have been inspected and recognised by the British Council. There are some schools which have been inspected and approved but have not joined ARELS-FELCO. As an association it can be very helpful to member schools both in an advisory capacity and for publicity. The organisation has for example produced guidelines for host families which many schools have used.

British Council Recognition is an indication of high standards in language courses, premises, welfare and accommodation. The British Council Recognition scheme is voluntary so there are also some good schools which do not have recognition.

For further information you may contact:

ARELS-FELCO Ltd.
2 Pontypool Place
Valentine Place
London SEI 8QF

1

What makes a holiday language course?

**1.0
A treasured memory**

The experience of travelling to and living in a foreign country without the support of parents is one which stays with a student for all his or her life. In a brief period of two or three weeks the student sees many new sights, hears new sounds, tastes new food, makes new friends and learns new ideas. It is a time, so rich in new experiences, that it will be remembered with more vividness than many years spent at school.

The truth of this statement will be recognised by any reader who enjoyed a similar experience as a child. The responsibility of those who work on holiday courses, is to feed the riches of this experience for the students and to fill those weeks with as many pleasant memories as possible.

A good holiday course is in the business of creating memories. The aim of this book is to help you to give the students an exciting and stimulating holiday, but one theme which will recur throughout the book, is the need to give the students concrete artifacts which will keep the memory alive.

**1.1
So you're going to work on a holiday course?**

This book is addressed to all those who work on holiday courses, language teachers, sports teachers, group leaders, social and excursions organisers and administrators. You will notice that the sections of this book focus on specific areas of responsibility. Although these sections are addressed to the specialists in the field, they are useful to all readers. Holiday courses involve a great deal of cooperation between specialists and so it is important that each person should understand what their colleagues are trying to achieve and their working procedures. You may have worked on holiday courses before and you will recognise some of the pitfalls which are described here. The book may help you to avoid some of the problems which you have not yet experienced. For those readers who are new to the field, this book will try to help you to enjoy your work and be as effective as possible.

Working on holiday courses can be the most tiring, frustrating, stimulating and rewarding periods of your life. Some holiday courses are well organised and the students get considerable benefit from their brief time in Britain. But, as holiday course directors will admit, their profession is not entirely populated by angels. Some holiday courses provide the minimum which will satisfy the students (and sometimes not even that!) but contribute little to their education or development.

Holiday course work will use all of the resources of your intellect and experience. If you are a teacher, your teaching duties will occupy a lot of your time, but you may well be asked to organise and supervise excursions to local monuments, judge disco-dancing competitions, comfort students who are homesick, discipline students who are unruly, take part in sports and talent contests, teach the highway code, collect 32 students arriving on three different delayed flights from Heathrow airport and, when you have just fallen asleep, get the boys out of the girls' dormitories.

The purpose of this book is to prepare you for this enjoyable ordeal. While you are working it will also serve as a reference at those moments when your brain has addled and you need some good ideas – or any ideas!

1.2
What will I be expected to do?

You may be employed as a 'teacher', but your responsibilities will extend far beyond the classroom. Even on a non-residential holiday course you will be the representative of the school whom the students will know best. They will automatically come to you with their problems so you will need to find out how these problems can be solved. These will range from students who are unhappy with their host families to the student who wants to buy a spare part for a film projector which a friend bought in England in 1962. You will be expected to be a fund of all knowledge and the source of all advice. So it is very important to know the accommodation and welfare officer, the person responsible for excursions, and so on.

On a residential course your day-to-day contact with the students will be much greater and you will probably be expected to help with excursions, airport transfers, sports and social activities. As mentioned above, you may also be responsible for supervising meals and getting the students to bed.

1.3
How will I help the student?

You can help the students to get the maximum benefit from their circumstances by the way you teach and the way you help in the organisation of the holiday course. You will help the students to develop friendships across a language barrier so that they will be obliged to use English for communication. You will organise sports teams, not as national teams – (Italy vs Spain), but by other criteria – (Reds vs Blues), so that even when practising sports, they are using their English. In organising excursions you will recognise the students' cultural background. You will not assume that students know the difference between Cardinal Wolsey and the Archbishop of Canterbury. You will not be shocked that students don't feel like eating 'toad-in-the-hole' or that they think the British are stupid to drive on the left. You will encourage the idea of adventure – an adventure in understanding.

1.4
The aims of the course
1.4.1
What is a holiday course?

The value of a holiday course is not measured only by the amount of new language which the students learn in the classroom. To calculate its value you must think of the totality of the experience. Indeed, for many students the greatest value is not gained through their classroom lessons but through contact and interaction with foreigners, the local people they meet and the students from other countries.

Holiday courses seek to combine aspects of a holiday with aspects of a language course. Holiday course organisations vary, some put their major stress on the 'holiday' but others concentrate on the language course. Frequently, students see the hours spent in a boring classroom as the 'price' they pay for the rest of the holiday. Getting the correct balance is not difficult, provided that you make the language course as enjoyable as possible and an integral part of the holiday.

1.4.2
Establishing the correct balance

As a learning experience the language classes are not the single most important element of a holiday language course. Some students will learn more through the social and cultural activities or the excursions than they will in the classroom. Sports teachers have the tremendous advantage that their words are often supported and demonstrated by actions so students will usually learn a lot during sporting activities. Many students will have to learn the tolerance and sharing which is required in residential accommodation or will experience, for the first time, life with a family of strangers. After many years of a diet of mother's cooking, students will be confronted with food which looks and tastes strange and alien.

All of these experiences serve to broaden the students' horizons and so all must be seen as being important. If you were to ask the students, they would probably say that accommodation and food were the most important aspect of the course, leisure activities would come second and lessons would be last! Their parents (your customers) might place the items in a different order, so whatever your speciality don't delude yourself that your work is the most important – every contribution to the development and well being of the students is ultimately important.

1.5
The Students
1.5.1
Who are the students?

There are holiday courses for students of all ages. This book is chiefly intended for those readers who will be working with children and teenagers, but it will also be useful to those who are working with adult students.

Holiday courses for young children are usually residential. Teenagers can choose between residential holiday courses and those which use family accommodation. There are a few residential holiday courses for adults but the majority use family accommodation or self-catering hostels.

Children are sent on holiday courses by their parents. The parents may not have any very clear idea of why they are sending the children but a holiday course does get rid of them for a time and fills up the overlap between the children's long holidays and the parents' annual four weeks.

Of course, many parents have more laudable motives. Maybe the child has done poorly at English classes at school and needs to improve. The parents may want the child to develop in maturity through contact with children of other nationalities.

The children are not responsible for their parents' motives, whatever they may be. It is your job to make those children as happy as possible during their holiday course, and, with luck, they may become more fluent in English.

There are holiday courses for adults and these present different challenges. Adult students come to learn or improve their English. They are usually paying for the course themselves and so they want to see results. The adult students' expectations of how much they will learn in a brief period are often ridiculous. You will have to show the students they are making progress even when they feel they aren't.

1.5.2 What do the students expect?

The students' expectations vary. Some imagine that they will be housed in luxury apartments, fed with haute cuisine food and entertained by show business giants. Others are more realistic.

Students often expect to be taught in the same way as they were taught when they were at school. This type of methodology may have been suitable for the circumstances which existed in the school but you will have to convince them that they should take full advantage of:-
(a) being in a class with students of other language groups
(b) being in an English speaking country.
Unfortunately, many holiday course teachers and students fail to exploit these advantages fully.

1.6 The Course Team

An essential element of a successful course team is a carefully defined structure of responsibilities. This serves to divide up the work which needs to be done and helps to prevent individuals from working themselves into a state of nervous exhaustion.

The organisational structure shown in the diagram on page 5 could exist in a large holiday course operation. Smaller centres would probably combine some positions – the Course Director may also serve as Director of Studies, the work of Social Director and Excursions Director may be done by a single individual. Often the Course Secretary may also be responsible for general welfare.

Very small centres may only be able to afford a single Director who is responsible for organising and supervising language classes, social activities, excursions, sports and welfare. At these centres, the teachers are involved in all aspects of the holiday course.

I have never seen such a slimmed down operation working successfully. By the end of the second week of the course both the director and the teachers are excessively tired, the quality of work suffers, teachers tend to become abrupt with students and to argue amongst themselves, coaches fail to arrive, activities are unsupervised and lessons become time-filling activities.

The structure of the course team needs to be adapted to the size of the holiday course operation. I have visited very large holiday course

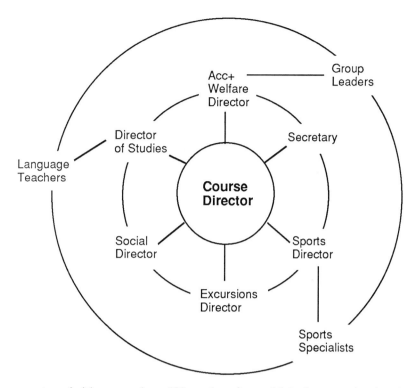

centres (with more than 500 students) at which the organisational structure
and administrative procedures were more suitable for a small centre. As a
result the staff did not know each other by sight, they had no idea of who
was responsible for organising or supervising the different activities. When
students had problems and asked their teachers for help, the teachers did
not know which members of staff could help to solve the problems.

1.6.1
The Course
Director

The Course Director has overall responsibility for the successful
management of the holiday course centre. He/She reports to the
headquarters of the holiday course operation. It would be difficult to list
all the Course Director specific responsibilities but the following list will
give an indication of the wide range.

- *to be ultimately responsible for the welfare and safety of both students
  and staff.*
- *to define and supervise the responsibilities of other staff members.*
- *to establish and maintain liaison between staff members.*
- *to establish and maintain discipline.*
- *to liaise with people not directly employed by the holiday course
  operation – caterers, coach companies, grounds staff, maintenance staff,
  etc.*
- *to administer budgets, reports and correspondence.*
- *to adjudicate in disputes concerning staff and students.*
- *to establish and operate procedures for quality control within the
  holiday course centre.*

| 1.6.2 The Director of Studies | The Director of Studies reports to the Course Director and is in charge of the language programme. He/She works closely with the Course Director and other members of staff to organise language classes and establish links between the language programme and other aspects of the holiday course. |

The Director of Studies reports to the Course Director and is in charge of the language programme. He/She works closely with the Course Director and other members of staff to organise language classes and establish links between the language programme and other aspects of the holiday course.

The Director of Studies' specific responsibilities would include:

- *testing and placement of students in classes.*
- *organisation of the class timetable.*
- *assigning teachers to classes.*
- *supervising the language content and teaching methodology of lessons.*
- *organising the assessment of the students' progress and attainment and the preparation of reports or certificates.*
- *assisting and advising language teachers.*
- *establishing and assisting procedures for liaison between language teachers to encourage the exchange of ideas and materials.*
- *establishing and maintaining beneficial links between the language programme and other activities.*
- *dealing with the complaints of students, national group leaders, teachers and others.*
- *all communications with students and other staff members concerning the language programme.*
- *establishing and maintaining procedures for quality control observation of lessons, etc.*

1.6.3 The Social Director

The Social Director is responsible for organising non-sporting entertainments and activities for the students during periods when they are not involved in language classes, sports or excursions. At most holiday course centres, the Social Director does not have staff who are specifically employed to assist with the social programme but liaises with the Course Director, Director of Studies and Sports Director to use language teachers, sports specialist and possibly group leaders to supervise social activities. The Social Director organises the Social Activities programme with careful consideration of the age and interests of the students, the possibilities offered by the site and the local area and the special talents of individual members of staff. He/She is also responsible for quality control of the social programme and must be prepared to adapt if the students are not enjoying the activities or being properly supervised.

The Social Director produces posters and other materials to promote the social programme and organises competitions, quizzes etc.

1.6.4 The Excursions Director

The Excursions Director is generally responsible for all activities which do not take place on site. Like the Social Director, the Excursions Director will probably use the resources of the language staff, the sports specialists and the group leaders to provide supervision of excursions. Through these supervisors, the Excursions Director is specifically responsible for the welfare and safety of students during excursions.

Apart from the normal cultural excursions, trips and shopping expeditions described in Chapter 6, the Excursion Director's responsibilities will include the transfer of students to and from airports on arrival and at departure (usually in association with the Course Director), sporting or social activities which take place off site and involving the use of coaches or taxis for transfer – ice skating, horse riding, visits to discos etc. (in association with the relevant directors), and the guided walking tour of the local area which is offered to new students on arrival.

The Excursions Director is responsible for organising and administering the excursions programme. Some destinations may have been pre-announced in brochures or other publicity materials and the Excursions Director should make sure that these promises are fulfilled. Selection of other destinations will depend on the interests of the students, the resources of the area and the finance available.

The Excursions Director is responsible for organising transportation, catering (if appropriate) and supervision for all excursions. In association with the Director of Studies and language teachers, he/she is responsible for the excursions noticeboard and the preparation of lectures, slide shows, worksheets and other materials which will help students to get the maximum benefit from the excursions.

1.6.5
The Sports
Director

The Sports Director leads the team of sports specialists and is directly responsible for the satisfactory planning and execution of the sports programme. In association with the Course Director and Director of Studies the Sports Director may also use some of the non-sports staff. As a leader of a team, the Sports Director will be responsible for assisting and supervising that team in the same way as the Director of Studies works with the language teachers.

The Sports Director organises and promotes the sports programme through posters, tournaments, competitions and so on.

He/She has overall responsibility for discipline and safety during all sports activities.

1.6.6
The
Accomodation
and Welfare
Director

The duties of the Accommodation and Welfare Director will differ in residential courses and those which use host family accommodation but in both the main tasks are to establish routines and to deal with any problems which arise.

On residential courses the Accommodation and Welfare Director will work with the catering and cleaning staff on site. He/She will probably use sports specialists, language teachers and possibly group leaders to help with the supervision of the students in the residences and during meals.

If the course uses host family accommodation he/she will be more concerned with selecting and working with the host families but may also be responsible for organising midday meals on site.

All staff who are in contact with the students have a welfare responsibility and the Accommodation and Welfare Director should encourage all staff to be aware of and to report on signs of homesickness or loneliness amongst the students.

He/She is also responsible for dealing with health problems amongst the students and will probably coordinate contacts with the local doctor.

<table>
<tr><td>1.6.7
The Course
Secretary</td><td>The importance of the work of the Course Secretary should never be underestimated. He/She helps the Course Director and other members of staff in an administrative and clerical capacity and will often supervise the school bank.</td></tr>
<tr><td>1.6.8
The Language
Teachers</td><td>The Language Teachers are directly responsible to the Director of Studies for all matters concerning the language lessons but outside these periods they will be asked to supervise meals, social activities, excursions and possibly sports and residential accommodation. Like the sports specialists they will spend many hours each day in close contact with the students and will therefore have an important welfare role.</td></tr>
<tr><td>1.6.9
The Sports
Specialists</td><td>The role of the Sports Specialists will be similar to that of the language teachers and the use of their talents will extend far beyond the confines of the sports field, tennis courts, swimming pool or gymnasium.</td></tr>
<tr><td>1.6.10
The Group
Leaders</td><td>The responsibilities of Group Leaders will vary considerably from one centre to another but it is important that the responsibilities are clearly negotiated and established. Although they may be involved in many different types of activities, their main concern will be discipline and student welfare.</td></tr>
</table>

2

The language teaching team

2.0
The members of
the team

Teaching English on a holiday course should be a learning experience for the whole team but if each member of staff prepares lessons individually and never discusses the work with the rest of the staff then there is little chance that much professional development will take place. A holiday course should be seen as an opportunity to learn new ideas, try out new techniques and eradicate bad habits. This can only be achieved by 'opening the classroom door' and allowing your colleagues to observe, criticise and suggest improvements. The Director of Studies has the major responsibility for this assistance but you will find that, because of their different backgrounds, the other teachers will also be capable of enriching your repertoire of classroom techniques.

This type of team needs some kind of organisational structure. There need to be clear lines of responsibility and provision for regular liaison and communication between teachers and with the Director of Studies.

2.1
The Director of
Studies

This position is given different titles in different organisations but for sake of brevity I will refer to the Director of Studies (DOS).

If you are appointed as a DOS you will probably be well qualified in EFL and will have some years' experience of teaching on holiday courses for the relevant age group. You will have a talent for organisation and managing people. You will have considerable tact and the ability to form a valid team from a group of teachers from varied backgrounds.

The DOS is rarely involved in the selection of teachers but is responsible for the management of the teaching team. This involves defining the responsibilities of individual teachers, supervising their lesson preparation, reports and classroom teaching. Since other directors may ask you to supply teachers as supervisors for other activities, you will have to make sure that the work is shared out fairly and your teachers are not allowed to become excessively tired.

The DOS is usually responsible for the testing of students and the formation of classes and timetables. There is also a major role in deciding the content of the language programme and managing resources such as classrooms, cassette recorders, cassettes, books, white board pens, card and so on.

The DOS has overall responsibility for the quality of the language programme. Your regular observation of lessons, staff meetings and contacts with students should allow you to do this.

2.2
The Teachers

Most holiday courses make a teacher responsible for one class of students. The class teacher is responsible for coordinating all the lessons, projects and homework tasks which are given to that class. Usually the class teacher will not do all the teaching for that class but will divide the work with another teacher.

In this way, each teacher works with two classes – as Class Teacher with one group and as Second Teacher with another group. As a Class Teacher, you will liaise with the Second Teacher to produce a weekly programme of work for your class. At the end of a lesson the teacher will make a brief note of the work done in the record book for the class together with any extra comments on individual students or aspects which require further development. As Class Teacher, you will be responsible (in collaboration with the DOS, the Second Teacher and other members of staff) for the preparation of the final report on each student so you should try to get to know your students very well. You should look out for signs of homesickness or other patterns of behaviour which will spoil the holiday course.

2.3
Adapting to holiday course teaching

Holiday course teachers are usually recruited from different groups:

(a) non-EFL teachers who normally work in state or private schools.

(b) Qualified EFL teachers who normally work overseas.

(c) Novices in the profession who have recently taken a short EFL course.

(d) University or College students who are training to be EFL teachers.

Each type of teacher brings a different type of expertise to the holiday course and needs to make different adaptations to his or her teaching style to accommodate the special conditions of the holiday course.

At this point you might like to skip to the section which deals with the category of teachers you belong to. (a) – 2.4, (b) – 2.5, (c) – 2.6, (d) – 2.7

2.4
British state and private school teachers

If you normally work within the British education system, you will be bringing many useful talents to the holiday course; your knowledge of child psychology and class management, your up to date experience of life and fashions in Britain and often special skills associated with the subject you normally teach. All of these talents are relevant to the holiday course, and if properly used will give your teaching a vigour and professionalism which your colleagues from other backgrounds may not be able to match.

The main area in which you will need to adapt will be language. You will probably have experience of teaching students who speak English as their second language but you should realise that the holiday course students' linguistic background is very different. Holiday course students have not been exposed to a daily diet of English on television, in the playground and in the classroom. They will not understand the idiomatic expressions and cultural references which your other students will take in their stride. The holiday course students' experience of English has been almost entirely through the school classroom where they have been taught a graded syllabus of language structures. They may be able to talk about the present and the past but have considerable difficulty expressing their ideas about the future. Their language will be very direct and they will be unable to express degrees of doubt or uncertainty.

When you speak to your holiday course students, you will have to use all your skills in assessing whether or not they have understood. You may have to be careful to speak more clearly than normal and to repeat and paraphrase your ideas. All experienced public speakers adapt their speed and clarity of speech to the size of their audience. Remember that Queen Victoria remarked, 'Gladstone speaks to Me as if I was a public meeting.' Since you will probably be accustomed to addressing classes of 30 students or more, the same style of speech will be suitable for the smaller classes of foreign students. Don't make the mistake of adopting your students' style of speech. It is very easy to drop into 'pidgin' English but this will not help your students in any way. If you have a strong regional accent, do not try to sound like a BBC newsreader but recognise that your students will take some time to get accustomed to your style of speech.

Before you start the holiday course, ask your employer if you can look at the types of teaching materials which the students will use. A quick way to understand their likely language experience is to read through some of the simplified, graded readers which are prepared at different levels. These will give you a good idea of the type of grammar and vocabulary they are likely to understand at each level.

When you are teaching the holiday course students, remember not to talk too much! In your normal work you are probably responsible for transmitting a certain body of knowledge. On the holiday course, the language itself is what you are trying to teach. So, make sure that you encourage the students to talk and interact with each other.

Your knowledge and skill in teaching your specific subject will also be useful. Remember that most holiday course students are still attending school at home and will probably be studying the subject which you teach. Whilst the content of Maths and Science programmes may be very similar all over the world, the teaching methodologies may be very different. The type of empirical approach widely used in Britain may be totally new to your holiday course students. History, Literature and Geography will certainly have a local flavour in each student's home country just as it does in Britain, but these differences in background should not deter you from using your specialist knowledge and skills with your holiday course students. Your subject can be a means through which your students acquire English so exploit the talents you have!

2.5
Qualified EFL teachers

If you are an EFL teacher who normally works abroad your knowledge of the system of the language and your teaching experience will be invaluable in your own lessons. You will be able to help your colleagues who may not have this background. You are probably accustomed to teaching monolingual classes and you may know the language which your students speak. This teaching situation offers certain advantageous aspects which will not be present in your holiday course classes. Even if you do not know your students' mother tongue, a little experience will soon allow you to predict the difficulties which they will find in studying some aspects of English.

If you know your students' mother tongue, you may be accustomed to using this resource when you are teaching. You will not be able to do this with multilingual classes on a holiday course.

You will have probably noticed the degree to which, in monolingual classes, the students help each other by translating what you have said to them. You may have tried to stop this but this perfectly natural behaviour certainly continues in a secretive fashion.

The monolingual class has certain disadvantages. Amongst the greatest of these is that the natural language of communication between the students will be their mother tongue and your attempts to make them interact in English will always be artificial.

You may be accustomed to teaching adults. You will find that children and adolescents learn in a different way and you will have to pay more attention to motivating the students with interesting activities.

Although you are a professional EFL teacher, do not imagine that you can teach on a holiday course in exactly the same way as you do normally. You have to remember that the students are only with you for a brief period and that they are on holiday! The aims of a holiday course teaching programme are different from those of a normal state school or a private language school so the style of teaching needs to be different.

The skills which you have acquired through training and experience will stand you in good stead on the holiday course provided that you adapt them to the special opportunities which the holiday course offers. You will have small multilingual classes and, with careful formation of pairs and groups, English will be the natural language of interaction. Take advantage of the fact that the English speaking world is just outside your classroom door. With so many opportunities for exposure to English around them it would seem a pity to isolate the students for hours in a classroom, so use the opportunities to take the students out.

Your background will enable you to help your colleagues from outside the EFL world but remember that you can also learn from them. Use the holiday course as an opportunity to share ideas. Write down the best ones so that you can use them when you get home!

2.6
Recently trained EFL teachers

If you are fresh from a short EFL teacher training course you will probably be full of ideas which you are eager to try out. Often some of these ideas will not be known by your colleagues so don't be inhibited by your lack of experience, share them with the other teachers.

You should recognise that holiday courses are very short and there is not enough time to teach everything. Set yourself reasonable teaching goals which can be achieved in the time available.

Your lack of actual classroom teaching experience will mean that you will need some help with discipline and classroom management. Read the advice to the untrained university or college students in the next section.

2.7 University or college students

If you are a university or college student the holiday course may be your first experience of real teaching. You will probably have the advantage of youth which the students will appreciate. Recognise that your youth is an advantage – many new teachers try to become middle-aged because they associate age with authority. You do not need to do this, your authority can be established through your voice and manner. Try to treat your students in the same way as you would treat your relatives of a similar age. You may well be frightened of the students during your first few lessons but try to avoid showing your fear. When a teacher shouts at a class, it is a clear sign that he or she has lost control. The students correctly interpret this and continue to make the teacher's life a misery. When you need to establish discipline, remember the power of the unblinking stare. Stillness and a firm voice convey more authority than shouting and rapid movement. If you are unsure of your ability to control the class and keep their attention ask your DOS for help. It may well be possible for you to watch one of the more experienced teachers in action. Steal as many ideas as you can. Nothing is really original in the world and we have all based our careers on stealing tricks from our colleagues.

Remember that students who are doing something cause much less trouble than those who are just sitting and listening. A lot of bad behaviour is caused by boredom so give your students plenty to do. You will have to be careful to give clear instructions and to check that they have been understood before the students start work. Students who don't know what to do cause as much trouble as those who are bored.

Careful planning is one of the best cures for nervousness. If you have planned a clear structure to the lesson and you know what you are trying to achieve you will overcome that dreadful fear of 'drying up' in front of the class but make sure that you have planned what the students will do rather than merely what you will do!

If you have been training to teach EFL you should have built up a good stock of ideas which you are eager to try out. If you don't have an EFL background you will have studied text books and readers as I have suggested above for teachers who normally work in state or private schools. The books listed at the end of Chapter 4 will also give you some ideas.

3

Administration

3.0 Administration of the language programme

The DOS is in charge of the administration of the Language Programme but the teaching staff will have to help with testing, keeping attendance registers, lesson planning and preparing reports.

Before the students arrive for the holiday course, the Course Director or Director of Studies will have made some decisions about the organisation of the language programme. How many lessons will the students have each day? How long will these lessons last? When will they begin and end? When, and for how long, will the students have a break? Will they have a snack during their break? How many different teachers will the students see each day? How many classes will there be? Will the classes be divided by language level, by age or both?

These decisions should take the following points into account. Younger students usually need shorter lessons and more space than older ones. Beginners need smaller classes than intermediate or advanced students. All students (except perhaps very young children) benefit from meeting as many different teachers as possible but each time a teacher moves from one class to another some working time is lost in both classes. A mid-morning break is important for both teachers and students. A snack will prevent them from losing concentration through hunger during the last lesson before lunch!

3.1 Testing and placement of students

The school will test the students in order to place them in classes. Language teachers are usually all involved in administering and grading. Tests can be highly sophisticated or very simple. It is most important to do an oral test as well as written tests. Many students, coming from a background of traditional grammar teaching, may perform very well on multiple choice grammar questions, but have little communicative oral ability. Since so much of the classwork will involve oral interaction, the students' oral skill and fluency may be more important than their knowledge of structure.

If you are asked to give an oral test, you can ask the student to tell you about their journey from their home country. This will require the student to use a wide range of vocabulary and structures. An alternative is to use a picture stimulus. It's quite easy to find illustrations or photographs which are open to various interpretations. Students can be asked to describe the pictures.

The easiest way to score an oral test is to use an ability scale such as the one below:

Level 1 Can only reply to simple questions with simple one word answers. Clearly has difficulty in understanding even simple questions.

Level 2 Can understand and reply to simple questions. Can make simple statements but frequently hesitates and makes grammatical, lexical and pronunciation errors. Has some difficulty in understanding slow, careful English speech.

Level 3 Can communicate reasonably well with a patient teacher but an average native speaker unaccustomed to 'foreign' English would find great difficulty in understanding and being understood. Speaks in short, direct, simple phrases.

Level 4 Can communicate well on a range of simple topics but makes many mistakes. Sometimes asks interviewer to repeat or explain the questions. Has difficulty talking about complex topics and expressing shades of meaning.

Level 5 Has no difficulty understanding interviewer and communicates well on most topics. Makes many mistakes but would be easily understandable to the average native speaker.

Level 6 Can communicate well on a wide range of topics. Is clearly not a native speaker but has considerable fluency and makes few mistakes.

Even though this system of grading oral ability may seem very simple, inexperienced EFL teachers should try to watch their more experienced colleagues administering and grading the test so that they agree about the grades.

The danger in most written or multiple choice tests comes from excessive confidence in the accuracy of the results. Teachers should always look carefully at the performance of each student in the class to see if that student has been placed incorrectly. It is very possible that with the excitement of a long journey and the strange experience of being in a foreign country, many students will under-perform so the school must have the flexibility to move incorrectly placed students during the first few days of lessons.

**3.2
Forming classes**

When forming classes the Director of Studies will be aiming to produce classes which are not too big, have a good mix of native languages, have students of similar age and have a fair uniformity of language level. The maximum class size should never exceed that stated in the school's publicity material. If there is the option to produce smaller classes, they should be formed at the lower end of the level spectrum and the lower end of the age range. The teachers will be doing a lot of student/student interaction, so a good language mix is as important as homogeneity of language level.

3.3
The classrooms and equipment

All the classrooms should be provided with suitable furniture. For most purposes, chairs with 'armrest desks' are most suitable. They can be easily moved for pair and group work and they do not occupy too much floor space. An over-crowded or badly furnished room puts severe limitations on good teaching. Every classroom needs a good board which can be seen by all the students. White boards are excellent provided that teachers are provided with the erasable water-based pens. There should also be a minimum of one audio-cassette recorder for each classroom. Remember that the students can use these machines for recording as well as listening to prerecorded cassettes. Some classrooms are subject to noise from traffic or other sources. If this is the case, it would be a good idea to close the windows for the few minutes that the students are listening to the cassette player.

The students' television room should be large enough to use as an extra classroom for working with videos. These may vary from published language teaching videos to commercial films or off-air recordings. Check the legal limitations on showing commercial video materials in schools. If the school or one of the teachers also has a video camera this can be put to very good use by the language teachers. It can also be used for introducing excursions and by sports staff for demonstrating games. (The videos can later be used as good promotional material for the school.)

3.4
The timetable

The number of hours of instruction offered will vary from school to school. When planning the timetable the DOS should make sure that all classes are taught by at least two different teachers. This, together with people who will be making announcements about sports and other activities will expose the students to a range of voices, accents and styles.

With the approval of the DOS, teachers might decide to vary the time when they concentrate on specific activities. If every morning starts with diary work followed by grammar revision the students will soon get bored by the routine. As mentioned in 4.7 below teachers should try to build as much variety into each week's programme as possible.

Student Register card

NAME *Marie Clare le Bolt*   ENTRY TEST *32/100*

CLASS *2A*

ARRIVAL *3/8* DEPARTURE *23/8*

| WEEK 1 | WEEK 2 | WEEK 3 | WEEK 4 |

DAY   ~~1~~ ~~2~~ ~~3~~ ~~4~~ ~~5~~   ~~1~~ ②③ ~~4~~ ~~5~~   ~~1~~ ~~2~~ 3 4 5   1 2 3 4 5

Comments

8/8/90 Very quiet and shy, but reads and writes well.
    TB
22/8/90 Has found friends, now more talkative.
        Her talent for drawing makes her
        popular in class.

Many schools use register cards for students which are clipped in a ring binder for each class. In this way the cards can follow the students as they move from one class to another.

3.5 Teaching materials

Because of the time needed to order books and cassettes and the financial restraints, it is rarely possible to give teachers a free choice of teaching materials. These will usually have been chosen by the DOS and teachers may have to ask for guidance in exploiting their assigned materials.

It is difficult to find good published teaching materials specifically written for holiday courses. Most course books are written for traditional school courses for use over a full school year. With the approval of the DOS, teachers should pick and choose within these books rather than attempt to work through unit by unit. If the teacher makes it clear to the students that this is going to be done, they will not feel that the teaching is unplanned.

There are materials published for short courses which can be used as the basis for a holiday course language programme. In addition to these there are a wide range of supplementary materials which concentrate on specific language skills.

Teachers should not feel that they are limited to published teaching materials. Newspapers and magazines are a good source of interesting and topical reading materials. Some can also make a useful stimulus for writing. The teacher's resource books listed at the end of Chapter 4 are a good source of ideas.

Also think about material which are linked to other activities on the course. If the students are going to visit Edinburgh Castle then any reading or listening material connected with the history of the castle will make the visit more interesting and valuable.

Remember that some materials will be available locally. Local guide books and newspapers are good sources. If the students read about a robbery at a bank in the High Street, they will be able to picture the scene and the reading will have more resonance.

4

The teacher prepares

This is not the place for a long dissertation on the processes of learning, but it is useful for all teachers to be reminded of current ideas.

Today, it is believed that students gain mastery of a language by two different processes. In the first process (which is called language acquisition), the student decodes the meaning of a piece of spoken or written language. The pattern of thought which was required to complete this process enlarges and enhances the student's capacity to decode and understand other messages. As the student is exposed to more and more comprehensible language, the capacity to comprehend develops quite unconsciously, without the intervention of a 'teacher'. In the context of the holiday course, the teacher should make sure that the students are exposed to a great deal of comprehensible language so that their ability to comprehend will be developed.

It has often been said that students will only learn to speak by speaking but the theory of language acquisition suggests that listening and reading are of greater importance. This being said, students will only develop confidence in speaking by being stimulated and given opportunities to speak in relaxed, unstressed conditions. On the holiday course, the language teachers and all the staff must develop the skill and patience to coax the shy, linguistically handicapped student to communicate in English.

The second learning theory is based on the principle of establishing (or 'imprinting') certain procedures or patterns of activity in the students' minds. Let's say that a teacher is trying to teach the students how to form questions in the Past Simple Tense. The teacher starts by demonstrating the procedure. The students are asked to follow and copy the teacher's steps. The teacher then gets the students to follow the same procedure repeatedly until, in theory, it is 'imprinted' in the students' minds.

What do you think students need?

How do you feel about the statements below? Your reactions will help you to systematise your philosophy of foreign language teaching on holiday courses.

1 The students have come to learn about the theories of language, they don't want to learn how to use it.

2 They are more interested in the English of past centuries than present day language and life.

3 Beware of making your lessons varied and interesting, students are inspired by boredom and monotony.

4 When they first arrive they feel relaxed, happy and secure.

5 They are accustomed to learning English in small, informal classes with students of many different nationalities and a teacher who is a native speaker of English.

6 Students love listening to the teacher's personal opinions, they don't want to express their own.

7 They prefer teachers who are stern and severe, they hate smiles and jokes.

8 They enjoy sitting at their desks in the classroom for hours every day. They don't want to move around or go out and experience English at work in shops, post offices, railway stations, etc.

9 They find it easier to understand reading and listening texts about obscure topics rather than subjects in which they have some knowledge and experience.

10 Students come to classes hoping that the teacher will ridicule all their mistakes and tell them that they are lazy and stupid.

11 Teachers should not apply any system of discipline until anarchy breaks out. It is easy to impose discipline when it becomes necessary.

12 Teachers who speak in strong clear voices should try to become as incomprehensible as possible. It is the only way students will gain a real command of English.

13 Teachers can assume that all students know how to express politeness in English.

14 Language classes should never refer to social activities, sports, excursions, accommodation, meals, or any other aspect of the holiday course.

15 Never decorate your classroom. The students prefer the pristine beauty of bare notice boards.

16 Unplanned lessons are usually relaxed and effective.

17 Teachers should always stick to the text book and never introduce materials which may be more relevant to the students.

18 Teachers should present themselves to their classes as all-knowing beings who are incapable of error.

19 All students remember the days when the Beatles were together and 1968 was a turning point in their youth.

20 The purpose of language classes is to occupy the students while the sports specialists and other staff relax and plan their activities.

Some people see a conflict between these two theories of learning but most would agree that both types of learning are used at different times. Language acquisition is clearly very important, but it is only through controlled practice activities that students will become accurate in their use of the language.

**4.1
Getting to know
the students**

In the first lesson tell the students a little about yourself and give them the opportunity to ask you questions. This will give you an opportunity to identify the most talkative and out-going students and an idea of the language level.

The first lesson is also the time for learning the students' names. Since they will also have to learn the names of their class mates, you can turn the activity into a competitive game.

It is probably a good idea to get the students to do a simple piece of writing in the first lesson. This is a quiet activity and the students will not feel excessively stressed. Ask them to write about their home town, their families or about their experience of learning English. Tell them that this is not a test and they should ask their class mates for help if they need it.

While the students are writing, move round and talk briefly with each of the students. This personal contact will help you to remember their names.

Collect in the pieces of writing but don't correct them. Keep them until the end of the course and then give them back to the students. This is a good trick for showing the students the progress they have made.

Try to end the lesson with a song or a simple game in order to stress that the course is going to be fun.

**4.2
The teacher's
behaviour**

Teachers learn certain tricks of behaviour which help them immensely when working with students. One concerns eye contact and visibility. If you can see all the students' eyes, then they can see you. Keep looking around the class and making eye contact with individual students. Regular eye contact is one of the keys to a friendly relationship.

Try not to remain too static in the classroom. It is very easy for the classroom to become divided into your 'territory' and the students' 'territory'. This stresses the distance between teacher and students and does not encourage close working relationships, so encourage the students to come to the front of the class to talk to the class, write on the board, etc.

Try to support what you are saying by using gestures and facial expressions. When you are writing on the board be careful not to block the students' view of what you are writing.

When speaking with the student, both in class and outside, use only English. You may be able to speak the native language of some of the students but please avoid the temptation to demonstrate your linguistic prowess. The students should think of you as a speaker of English and use only English when communicating with you.

**4.3
Teacher
domination**

It is very easy for a teacher to become excessively dominant in the classroom. This tendency to dominate is often the result of nervousness or a feeling that if you are not 'teaching' the students are not learning. The students will learn through what *they* do, not through what you do. Your job is to create conditions in which they will learn. If they spend the whole lesson listening to your voice they will learn very little. If they spend the lesson being active, they will learn a lot more.

4.4
Errors and
correction

Students make errors when their desire to communicate goes beyond their linguistic ability. An error is an indication that the student wants to use the language. A teacher should never laugh at or criticise a student for making an error. Always praise the effort before you correct the error. 'Yes, very good Sandro, but . . .'

You should not interrupt a student to correct every error. If the activity is one which concentrates on accuracy, you will probably want to correct more of the mistakes. If the activity is more concerned with communication, then you would only highlight those errors which inhibit communication. You should remember to tell students when you want them to concentrate on accuracy and when they should try to be fluent.

Don't be too eager to correct the errors yourself. Try to get the student who made the error to correct it, if not then ask one of the other students. Try to create an atmosphere in the classroom in which the students are not frightened of making mistakes. Students who don't make mistakes usually don't make anything!

4.5
Making the
classroom a
place of learning

Holiday course lessons may take place in study bedrooms in a university college, in small rooms in a Church Hall or, if you're lucky, in a purpose built classroom. Whatever the setting, you will probably find that any decorations have been stripped from the walls, notice boards are bare and the only reading materials in the room are the scratchings and carvings of generations of bored students.

If you are going to teach in a room such as this, you should try to make it a little more attractive and stimulating for the students. A few posters will soon brighten up the room. Even the obligatory instructions for evacuation in case of fire will provide some reading material. Start by putting up a few posters and notices. Make little displays of frequent questions the students might ask – 'What does X mean?', 'How do you spell X?', 'Can you tell me the time, please?', 'What time does it start?', 'Can you repeat that please?' A friend of mine always has a large decorated 'S' on the wall. When students drop the 's' from third person singular forms of present simple verbs, he just points to the 'S' to remind the students. Depending on the level of the class, you might make displays of vocabulary – colours, food, sports, sizes (from tiny to gigantic), faces showing emotions, pictures of pop or film stars used to illustrate descriptive language – 'She has long blonde hair and blue eyes'. The potential is endless.

These materials will not only make your classroom a more attractive place but also allow the students to 'learn from the walls' even when you are not there!

Before the students arrive, you should make a start with these decorations but most of the work can be done by the students themselves.

While the students are looking through old magazines trying to find a picture to illustrate, for example, 'angry', they will pick up a lot of incidental language exposure.

Use the noticeboards in the classroom for displays of your students' work. An early display project could be for each student to write a brief autobiography and attach a photograph. The other students in the class will be eager to read these and you will have started the habit of reading from the noticeboards. Another display idea starts from a world map, the students write about their home towns. These texts are displayed beside the map with a pin showing where the town is situated. The possibility of display is a strong source of motivation for students. These displays can include the results of their projects as well as stories, diary reports, poems, jokes and other materials.

If you can, try to decide on different seating plans for the classroom. Unless the desks and chairs are screwed to the floor, you should be able to move the furniture to suitable positions for different types of activity – pairwork, group work, role plays and so on. The students will appreciate the change and will approach their work with greater enthusiasm.

4.6 Homework

Many holiday course organisations have found that giving students homework has very beneficial results. On residential courses a quiet period in the evening is often devoted to supervised homework. You should beware of the temptation to set boring, repetitive tasks for homework. We are always concerned to make our lessons as interesting and stimulating as possible, but we often make the mistake of setting boring homework tasks. Some students like repetitive pattern practice because it makes them feel secure, but you should try to give a choice to those students who would prefer to do something more creative. Silent reading is always useful and if the school has a good stock of graded readers, the students might prefer to read.

4.7 Planning a week's programme

If you are sharing the teaching of a class with a colleague, you should always work together on the plan of a week's learning programme. This will obviously help to avoid duplication of work and prevent the students from being given two similar lessons (e.g. reading comprehension) one after another.

In planning a week's programme you should aim to include most or all of the different types of work listed in section 5.2. Remember that some types of work require more time than others. Project work takes a lot of time and is less enjoyable if it has to be rushed. When deciding on the amount of time to be devoted to each type of work, try to think in terms of the learning value for the students. Beware of spending too much time on songs and games unless you are sure of their learning value. Students certainly enjoy songs and games and they should be included in any programme of lessons, but try to use the songs and games to help the students learn or practise the language, rather than simply to entertain them.

Generally with young or low level students you should aim for a greater number of shorter activities because they will have less stamina than older or more proficient students. A good advanced class can happily spend an entire lesson on a reading passage because they will study it in considerable depth. Lower level students will only be looking at the surface meaning of very short texts.

The week's programme should provide for variety within each day's activities. Recognise that your students' ability to concentrate will change during the day. If you are starting the morning's lessons, begin with some warm up activities such as choral speaking to help the students to wake up. The first lesson of the day should always include some oral interaction. If students start the day with silent writing activities (like diary work) they often tend to be unresponsive for the rest of the lessons. Holiday course students are frequently tired in the mornings because they have spent half the night talking after 'lights out'.

The lessons within the weekly plan should follow a logical sequence. The plan should not consist of a collection of unrelated lessons. Skills learnt in one lesson should be practised in another. New words learnt from a reading passage should be recycled later in the week in some sort of vocabulary activity. Try to make each day refer back to the previous day's lessons and lead in to the next day's lessons. The more links which you develop between class activities and other non-academic activities during the holiday course the better.

Each day should include some grammar revision, some vocabulary work, some reading or listening comprehension, some oral interaction and some opportunities for creativity. Creative activities can include writing (creative writing not guided composition), role plays or for lower level students drawing or illustrating a scene from a story which they have read.

4.8 Planning a lesson

Lesson planning is essential in order to ensure that:

- *Time is not wasted.*
- *Activities are not interrupted by the end of the lesson.*
- *All the necessary equipment is available.*
- *There is sufficient variety.*
- *The lessons are not teacher dominated.*

This last point is particularly important. It is very easy for inexperienced teachers to make plans for what the teacher will do in each lesson without thinking about the lesson from the students' viewpoint. It is better to plan the students' lesson and then to add notes on the teacher's actions.

Each lesson should have clearly defined learning aims. Do not confuse these aims with students' activities. The aim of doing an exercise is not inherent in the exercise itself but in what the students learn from the exercise.

During the students' school year, English lessons are preceded and followed by lessons in other subjects which are probably taught in their mother tongue. On holiday courses the English lessons are not sandwiched between lessons in other subjects and so the techniques of lesson planning need to be somewhat different. Remember to think from the students' point of view. Although they may only be taught by you for an hour, they will be doing a three or four hour English lesson each day. The need for variety within and between lessons is particularly important if the students are not to become bored.

As suggested above the selection of activities for each lesson should be related to the students' ability to concentrate at different periods in the day. Try to alternate high and low intensity activities gradually increasing the time devoted to low intensity activities towards the end of the morning.

Don't make the mistake of assuming that high intensity activities are always 'serious' work like written exercises, oral drills or dictations. Some language games in which all the students are involved and which require quick reactions are very high intensity activities because they are mentally very demanding. If the work is associated with the students' own lives it will be more enjoyable and memorable.

Each lesson period of 40–50 minutes should contain at least eight different activities at beginners' level, six activities at elementary or pre-intermediate levels and four activities at intermediate or advanced levels. The last activity before a change of teachers or the end of the teaching day should have a high 'entertainment' element which will make the students look forward to the next lesson with that teacher.

After each lesson the teacher should think about the following questions:

- *Did the students achieve the objectives of the lesson?*
- *Were ALL the students actively involved in the lesson?*
- *Did ALL the students participate in the lesson?*
- *Did the lesson link back to previous lessons and forward to future lessons?*

**4.9
The teacher
resource pack**

Although the holiday course organisation should supply most of the stationery and books you will need, you may wish to bring some materials to make your teaching more personal and effective. Pictures and other visual materials are always useful particularly if they relate to your students' age range or your own special interests. Many teachers have pictures or toys which they use in their teaching. A pack of standard playing cards can have a wide range of uses. Picture cards (or post cards) for teaching vocabulary would be useful at beginner elementary level. Examples of project work done by other students are often a good stimulus for reluctant students. You may also want to bring your guitar or recordings of favourite songs to teach the students.

**4.10
Books to read
and refer to**

Most holiday courses have a small library of methodology and reference books for teachers but frequently teachers find that they do not have the time to consult them so try to get hold of some of the following books and read them before you start work.

The Practice of English Language Teaching by Jeremy Harmer (Longman) one of the best general methodology books for all teachers.

Techniques for Classroom Interaction by Donn Byrne (Longman) a rich variety of interaction activities which can be adapted to all levels.

Fitting In Edited by Jimmie Hill (LTP) an introduction to British life for foreign students. An excellent resource for relevant communicative language work.

Games for Language Learning by Andrew Wright, David Betteridge and Michael Buckby (CUP) the best source of valuable language learning games available.

The Q Book by John Morgan and Mario Rinvolucri (Longman) Questionnaire based activities for vocabulary development, grammar practice and communication.

Have You Tried This? 1 & 2 by Jim Wingate (Pilgrims) two collections of successful lesson ideas from Pilgrims' summer courses.

Grammar in Action by Christine Frank and Mario Rinvolucri (Prentice Hall) supplementary grammar activities for elementary and intermediate students.

Once Upon a Time by John Morgan and Mario Rinvolucri (CUP) story telling techniques for teachers with more than 50 skeleton stories to exploit.

Grammar Games by Mario Rinvolucri (CUP) more language games with an emphasis on grammar.

1,000 Pictures for Teachers to Copy by Andrew Wright (Collins) a simple training course in drawing for teachers.

Teaching Oral English by Donn Byrne (Longman) one of the classics of EFL methodology.

Teaching Writing Skills by Donn Byrne (Longman) another classic, the best book on this topic.

Developing Listening Skills by Shelagh Rixon (Macmillan) a practical guide for classroom teachers at all levels. Includes a guide to exploiting your own material.

Teaching Reading Skills in a Foreign Language by Christine Nuttall (Heinemann) theories of reading are explained and demonstrated.

Vocabulary by John Morgan and Mario Rinvolucri (OUP) over a hundred vocabulary based learning activities for a variety of levels.

Teaching and Learning Grammar by Jeremy Harmer (Longman) a simple practical guide to teaching grammar.

Practical English Usage by Michael Swan (OUP) an accessible guide to English grammar illustrating typical student errors and correct usage.

Longman English Grammar by L. G. Alexander (Longman) a new general reference grammar for teachers and advanced students.

Longman Dictionary of Contemporary English (Longman) an intermediate/advanced level dictionary for language learners which is also valuable for language teachers.

Longman Dictionary Skills Handbook by Janet McAlpin (Longman) a collection of dictionary training exercises.

5

Aims and methods

**5.0
Aims – finding
the correct
balance**

Most students who come on holiday language courses also learn English at
school in their own countries. Therefore they have some expectations of
what studying a language should be like. In many respects the style of
teaching they have experienced is unsuitable for learning the language on
a holiday course because it fails to exploit the students' exposure to
English outside the classroom.

However, you should not ignore the students' expectations (even if
you consider them mistaken) because it is important that they feel that the
work is useful.

Thus the main aim is to find the correct balance between the
students' notions of language learning and activities which will actually
exploit the situation.

**5.1
The special
opportunities of
a holiday course**

If we compare a school classroom in the students' home countries with a
holiday course classroom, we can see some of the special opportunities
which the holiday course offers.

(a) *Individual attention*

A smaller class offers increased individual attention from the teacher
and greater possibilities for less rigid interaction activities.

(b) *Natural use of English in interaction*

In a class where all the students speak the same mother tongue, it is
very unnatural for them to speak to each other in English. In a
multilingual class, such as you usually find on holiday courses, the use
of English is much more natural and spontaneous. So the holiday
course offers unrivalled opportunities for student/student interaction
activities, role play, simulations, project work and so on.

(c) *Constant exposure to English*

When the students are learning English as part of their school curriculum they will go from their English lesson to a lesson given in their native language. There is no continuity of exposure to the foreign language. While they are on the holiday course they will be exposed to English for ten or more hours each day. This exposure will mean that the students take less time to switch into English when they begin their lessons and will have ample opportunities to practise between lessons.

(d) *English in the classroom and outside*

English teachers in the students' home countries have little motivation to take the students outside the classroom because the environment does not naturally stimulate the use of English. Teachers on holiday courses have very good reasons to take the students out of the classroom because they have a whole world of stimuli within easy reach.

(e) *Integration with other activities*

Teachers often complain at the lack of 'content' in their language lessons. On a holiday course, there are many opportunities to integrate language work with excursions, sports, competitions and cultural activities. This integration provides the required content so that students are not talking and writing about the activities of fictitious characters from their text books but their own past, present and future activities. The students are more strongly motivated by these topics.

**5.2
Learning goals**

We all recognise the difference between learning and teaching. Learning takes place both in the classroom and outside because the students observe, understand and remember new bits of language. Unfortunately, we also know that sometimes teaching takes place without learning!

During the two or three weeks of a holiday course, the students will learn an enormous amount by interacting with the sports teachers, host families and with students from different language groups because they have to use English for communication. In that same brief period, we cannot expect to improve radically the students' knowledge of language structures.

Our major aim should be to consolidate the language which the students have 'half learnt' at school. We will also aim to develop the students' fluency in the use of this language.

Our specific linguistic goals will probably lie in the following areas:

Pronunciation

We should aim to develop the students' perception of the sounds of English and from this improve their pronunciation, their use of stress and intonation.

Pronunciation

1 *Remember the schwa!*

This is the most important vowel sound in English. It is used at the end of all your favourite relatives – mother, father, brother, sister, daughter but not son!

2 *Learn to use weak forms*

Students think they are speaking correctly when they give each vowel its full value. Teach the students to use natural weak forms.
What's the difference in pronunciation between the two words underlined in these exchanges?

A I <u>was</u> there but Tim wasn't
A I <u>can</u> swim but Tim can't
B Yes, I <u>was</u>!
B Yes, I <u>can</u>!

3 *We don't spell what we say*

Which letters are not heard in these words?

Coastguard, Comfortable, Friends, Awfully

4 *There is no white space between words*

Speech is a more or less continuous stream of sound. There are not gaps of silence between words. The words run into each other. Think of the sound of these phrases.

Pick it up. I'm a manager. He wants an egg.

5 *Listen to stress in words*

Students will often put the stress on the wrong syllable in words. Think about the stress in these words.

o O   O o
Can I record your record?

o   o o
Are you sitting comfortably?

6 *Do you go up or down?*

Intonation is very important in conveying mood and meaning.
Glide Down – starts high and glides down.
How do you think we ought to start?
The train was late.

29

Glide Up – starts at medium level and glides up at the end.
Have they arrived yet?
Are you married?

Take-off – starts and continues low but rises at the end.
I was only trying to help.
No one's stopping you.

The Dive – Starts from high, falls to low and then rises to middle.
I may be able to come on Wednesday.
Don't worry!

7   *Practise pronunciation with minimal pairs*
Minimal pairs are pairs of words which sound exactly alike apart from one key sound.

ship : sheep, chip : cheap, slit : sleet, pen : ben, peat : beat, post : boast

8   *Books to consult*

Teaching English Pronunciation by Kenworthy (Longman)
Better English Pronunciation by O'Connor (CUP)

9   *Read pronunciation in your dictionary*

If your students learn to read the international phonetic alphabet they will be able to check pronunciation in their dictionaries.

CONSONANTS		VOWELS	
These symbols are used for both the British and American pronunciations:			
Symbol	Key Word	Symbol	Key Word
p	pack	e	bed
b	back	æ	bad
t	tie	iː	sheep
d	die	ɪ	ship
k	class	ɑː	calm
g	glass	ɒ	pot
tʃ	church	ɔː	caught, horse
dʒ	judge	ʊ	put
		uː	boot
f	few	ʌ	cut
v	view	ɜː	bird
θ	throw	ə	better
ð	though	eɪ	make
s	soon	əʊ	boat
z	zoo	ɑɪ	bite
ʃ	shoe	aʊ	now
ʒ	measure	ɔɪ	boy
		ɪə	here
m	sum	eə	hair
n	sun	ʊə	poor
ŋ	sung		
h	hot	eɪə	player
l	lot	əʊə	lower
r	rod	ɔɪə	employer
j	yet	aɪə	tire
w	wet	aʊə	flower

Social skills

We should take the students' 'raw' survival English and teach them how to add the formulae of politeness. We should teach them to listen and how to 'take turns' in a conversation.

Study skills

We should both teach new vocabulary and the skills for memorising and mastering new words. We should give guidance in planning and organising their written work and in using dictionaries effectively.

Oral skills

Small classrooms offer splendid opportunities for developing confidence in spoken communication. In some classrooms students only react to spoken English by answering the teacher's questions. On a holiday course we should help the students to develop the skills and confidence to initiate interactions and conversations.

Questions

1 *Yes/No Questions*
Is she still in bed?
Does she like apples?
Have they seen that film?

Yes/No questions can be used to check comprehension. They are very easy for students because they require minimum response.

2 *Either/or questions*
Do you want to go to Brighton or Hastings?
Are they swimming or skating?
Was it hot or cold?

Either/or questions are slightly more demanding than Yes/no questions. Remember that short answers – 'Hastings', 'Swimming', 'Cold' are more natural than so-called 'full' answers.

3 *'Wh' Questions*
Where are they going?
What can you see?
Why did you do that?

'Wh' questions are used for eliciting information. They are usually formed by inverting the statement form
They are going. Where are they going? but be careful with 'who'
They saw the man. Who saw the man? Who did they see?

4   *Encourage the students to ask questions*

Show the students a picture or let them read a text and then get them to ask questions. Why not use a question matrix like this and play noughts and crosses (tic, tac, toe)?

Who?	*Where?*	*Whose?*
What time?	*What?*	*What colour?*
How old?	*Which?*	*How many?*

5   *Ask a silly question – and you will look a fool!*

Teachers often ask silly questions because they want to elicit specific answers but this just confuses students.

Have I got two heads?
Anna, are you a girl?
What's your name, Marco?

6   *What's the date today? . . . José*

When addressing the whole class always ask your question, then pause before naming the student who should respond. In this way all the class will think of the answer to the question. Avoid asking questions around the class in a set pattern. The students will soon learn the pattern and go to sleep as soon as they have answered.

Maintenance skills

Since we want the students to retain the skills we are giving them, we will also teach maintenance skills – how to approach ungraded reading and listening texts.

As will be seen from the above we will not be aiming at a continuation of the type of work which the students usually do at school, but concentrating on the special opportunities which a holiday language course can offer.

**5.3
Classroom
activities**

Now that we have established our learning goals for the students, we need to consider the types of classroom activities which we will use to achieve these results. The purpose of the teaching methods we use is not always immediately obvious to the learners. Most young children are given crayons and colouring books. The purpose of this is partly to keep them quiet, but the real educational value comes from the development of hand/eye coordination and muscle control. Of course we don't tell a four year old that his or her hand/eye coordination and muscle control are improving, we say 'That's a lovely picture!' However your students are sufficiently mature to be told why they are asked to do a particular exercise or activity.

**5.4
Communicative
language**

Students on a holiday course in an English-speaking country will have immediate needs for communicative language. When they are at school in their home country they will not use English outside the classroom and therefore when, for example, they learn how to ask for something politely in English, there will be no immediate need or opportunity to use that language. On a holiday course, the students will have opportunities to use new language immediately after the lesson.

This gives the students a strong motivation to learn this type of language because it can help them to overcome recognised communicative barriers. *Fitting In*, a small book published by Language Teaching Publications, provides an excellent analysis of the most frequent communicative needs of the foreign student. The analysis is similar to that seen in traditional 'phrase books' but the students are helped to learn and adapt key phrases to different situations.

As will be mentioned later in this book, the problems which occur in relations between foreign students and local people are often linguistic in origin. Host families often say that their foreign guests sound rude and 'abrupt'. This is because students have learnt the most simple exponent of common functions and these often sound rather rude. Consider the difference in politeness between:

More tennis balls!
Give me more tennis balls!
Can you give me some more tennis balls, please?
Could you give me some more tennis balls, please?

You will notice that the more polite phrases in English, tend to be structurally more complex.

Probably the easiest way to organise a lesson on this type of language is to use a situational approach. Select a situation such as 'at the breakfast table', and then ask the students for all the words they know which might be used in this situation. Write these words on the board and check that all the students understand the meanings. Then ask the students to suggest phrases which might be used. Again write these on the board. You will have prepared a list of suitable phrases yourself and at this point, you can add them. You should do some choral practice of these key phrases using

Communicative Language

The list of situations suggested below is by no means complete but will provide a starting point.

At the table
Offering, accepting and refusing.
Requests.
Expressing likes and dislikes.
Commenting on food.

Shopping
Asking about prices.
Cheap/Expensive.
Asking to buy things.
Talking about money.
Buying things.
Talking about sizes, materials, etc.

Asking directions
Inside a building.
In the town.
Asking about transport.
Asking about times.

On Excursions
How old? How far? How many? etc.
Asking for repetition/clarification.

Thanking
Thanking for gifts.
Thanking for actions.
Different levels of intensity.

Making conversation
Starting a conversation.
Talking about your home and family.
Talking about your region.
Talking about your work/school.
Talking about your habits.

Meeting people
Greetings at different times of day.
Greetings at different levels of formality.
Talking about the weather.
Parting remarks.

Bathrooms, toilet, etc.
Asking permission.
Asking about availability.
Asking location.
Euphemisms – loo, lavatory, rest room, etc.
Soap, towels, toothpaste, lavatory paper.
Hair dryers, electric razors, etc.

Sports
Winning and losing.
Talking about ability/inability.
Instructions.
Asking for, giving and refusing permission.

Apologising
Excuse me, Sorry, I'm afraid . . . .
Different levels of intensity.

Illness
Talking about how you feel, aches, pains, etc.
Asking to be excused actions.
Requesting actions.

the vocabulary which you collected before. During the choral practice, draw the students' attention to the intonation of the phrases. Intonation is a most important indication of politeness in English.

You will stress the use of 'please' and 'thank you', those magic words which lubricate interpersonal relationships in English. Make some comments about facial expressions. Foreigners, with their limited command of the language, need to use the communicative force of facial expressions to add meaning to the words they use. If *you* have lived in another country, you will have noticed how much more you need to smile and use gestures.

In the next phase of the lesson the students might try to role play a scene at a breakfast table, using the new language they have learnt. In groups, they could also write a dialogue which has this setting. An alternative would be for you to give them an impolite dialogue and ask them to make it more polite.

Obviously, this type of approach can be treated at different language levels according to the ability of the students. You can also use a range of materials including text books and videos as a starting point for this type of work.

In the chapter on accommodation, the 'Arrival Pack' for students staying with host families is described. You can develop this type of communicative language as well, because you want the students to talk to their host families.

5.5 Grammar revision

Students will expect that some grammar work will be done during the course. During a holiday course you will not have time to do more than 'half teach' any new structures so in the grammar revision lessons you should concentrate on developing understanding and accuracy in the use of those patterns which students have 'half learnt' at their normal schools. Remember that all the students will have different areas of knowledge and ignorance. If you can bring the whole class to the same level of knowledge, then every student will have made a significant advance.

If you have little experience of teaching English to foreign students, you will find that L. G. Alexander's *Longman English Grammar* provides very clear guidance and explanation.

Many published courses and supplementary texts contain grammar revision. You will probably find one which will suit the level of your students. Most of the work will be done by drawing from the students' knowledge, rather than trying to pump them full of new knowledge. The basic procedures are identification, interpretation, construction, manipulation, practice and production.

In the IDENTIFICATION and INTERPRETATION phases you can present a dialogue or reading passage which contains examples of the key structure. After guiding the students to a global understanding of the text through questions, you can focus their attention on one example of the structure and check that they understand the meaning. Then you can ask them to identify the other examples of the same structure in the text. Again you would check comprehension. You could also write some isolated phrases on the blackboard and ask the students to create short dialogues in which the phrases might appear.

In the CONSTRUCTION phase the students will help you to complete a paradigm or 'grammar box' showing the construction of the pattern. This will develop into the MANIPULATION phase in which students will show how the pattern changes from singular to plural and in question and negative forms. There are many books of PRACTICE excercises. Since you are doing grammar revision you should try to do these exercises at high speed.

Language games provide an amusing context for the PRODUCTION phase of the lesson. Of course, the real communicative production of these structures will take place in other lessons and outside the classroom, but language games are usually short and fun. Your colleagues will know some language games and you can find many others in *Games for Language Learning* and *Grammar Games* (both published by Cambridge University Press) and other collections of language games.

5.6 Vocabulary development and dictionary work

During the holiday course students will meet lots of new vocabulary. Your aim will be to train the students in the skill of guessing the meanings from form and context. If students ask you the meaning of a word from a reading passage, avoid giving them an immediate explanation. Ask them what they think it means. Does it look like or sound like another word in English or in another language they know? Is the word a noun, a verb, an adjective – what is it? Always try to use questions to guide the students towards finding the meaning for themselves. When they have done this let them check their deductions in their dictionaries.

Vocabulary

1 *Passive and active*

We all understand more words than we use. This is true of native speakers and foreign learners. Words in our PASSIVE vocabularies (which we understand but do not use) will only become ACTIVE if there are occasions when we *need* to use them and we are confident of knowing *how* to use them.

2 *Beware of lists!*

Students are often encouraged to make word lists but words die in lists! They *live* in meaningful sentences and utterances. If students have 'vocabulary books' for new words, tell them to write example sentences beside each word (rather than the translation). Alphabetical lists are less useful than lists which group words by topic or situation.

3 *Words and feelings*

Students are more likely to remember words which they have strong feelings about so ask them to produce displays of

FIVE THINGS I LIKE BEGINNING WITH 'G'.

FIVE THINGS I HATE BEGINNING WITH 'S'.

4 *Illustrate the meanings of words*

minuscule tiny small medium large gigantic

---

5   *Strong emotions give meaning to your lines!*

Discuss with students the meaning of emotion words like happy, sad, confused, angry, frightened, shy, calm, etc. Ask the students to divide a piece of paper into four or six rectangles. Ask them to choose an emotion word from the board and then draw a line which illustrates that emotion. Then they should choose another word and draw another line until all the rectangles are full. Then the students should exchange papers and try to identify which word matches each line.

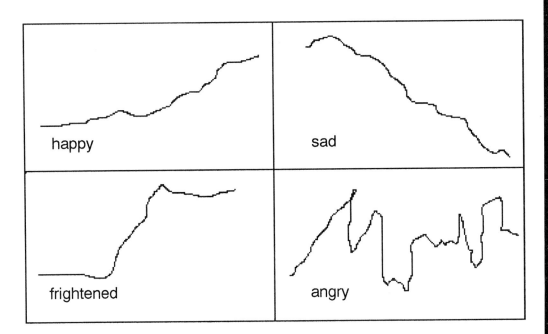

This is developed from an idea from Andrew Wright. You will find a wealth of good ideas in his books.

6   *Vocabulary research activity – colours*

Send the students out of the classroom in teams after giving each team a colour. Tell them to stay on the school premises and to come back in 10 minutes. Ask them to make a list of as many things as they can see which are their given colour. Let them use their dictionaries. When they come back, they have to explain to the others what they have seen.

7   *Game – I don't know the word for . . .*

One of the most important survival skills for foreign students is the ability to 'explain around' words which they do not know. Monolingual dictionaries for language learners do this by physical description or function. Then ask students to explain a 'horse' without using the word! Can their colleagues guess what they mean?

8   *Do you want some more ideas?*

Vocabulary by John Morgan and Mario Rinvolucri (OUP) contains lots of ideas and activities for vocabulary development.

Much of this new vocabulary will be soon forgotten unless you can teach the students how to retain it. Students often keep note books in which they write new items of vocabulary (sometimes with the translation in their mother tongue beside each entry). Some students simply list the words as they meet them, others put them in alphabetical order with a page devoted to each letter. A more useful arrangement is by topic so that, for example, all words connected with sports are listed together.

You should spend some time training the students to see each new word not as a single item to be learnt but the starting point for a voyage of discovery. A dictionary will give the meaning of the word, its grammatical form and perhaps its opposite. A thesaurus will list words which are related in meaning. Tom McArthur's *Longman Lexicon of Contemporary English* gives dictionary explanations of words but is organised in semantic fields. In this way a student who looks up 'castle' will find 'tower', 'keep' and 'moat' in the same section.

Pocket bilingual dictionaries are very popular with holiday course students and many will bring them from home. These are a useful 'safety net' for students but they are of very little value for foreign language learning. More useful are the range of monolingual dictionaries specifically designed for language students.

Most students have never been trained to use dictionaries and consequently never read beyond the first line of a dictionary entry and do not understand much of the information contained. Many monolingual dictionaries for language learners now have workbooks with exercises for dictionary training.

Students remember words which they use, so when they are writing in their scrapbook diaries they should try to use the new words which they have learnt. You will be encouraging the students to talk about their activities outside the classroom and you should praise them when they use new words.

Some of your lessons should be devoted to vocabulary development. Try to use topics which are immediately related to your students' experiences on the holiday course. If they are going to visit a castle, you can use this as your starting point for a vocabulary search. Elicit as much vocabulary as you can from the students, you may have to prompt them (Yes, knights used to live in castles. What did they wear when they were fighting? What did they fight with?). The effect of relating classroom vocabulary development to the holiday course will be to make the vocabulary much more vivid and memorable.

Remember that they can also do vocabulary development for homework. Ask the students, for example, to find the names of five types of food which they like or five different ways of preparing food.

**5.7
Skills
development**

A holiday course provides an excellent opportunity for developing the four major language skills; listening, reading, speaking and writing. Much of the work which is done can be integrated with other activities taking place on the holiday course. You will be able to use authentic materials which are of immediate interest to the students. You can read about and discuss excursions which are planned. The sports staff may want the students to read and understand the rules of behaviour in the swimming pool. You can record (or ask other members of staff to record) announcements about competitions or tournaments and use them for listening comprehension. Students (of any level) can produce posters advertising forthcoming events.

Listening

1 *Spiral comprehension*

   Start with general questions which will help students to gain a general impression of the setting, speakers and content:

   Who is speaking? How many people? Young or old? Male or female? Mood – angry, calm, excited, frightened?

   Where are they speaking? Listen for key words and sound effects.

   What are they talking about?

   Then listen again for more specific information:

   What time did she arrive? Where had she come from? Why was she late?

2 *Ask questions first*

   Always ask your questions before the students listen to the recording so that they will know what information to listen for. You can even ask students to suggest possible answers before they hear the recording.

3 *No good at listening? (1)*

   Students often find listening difficult because they try to understand every word. This makes them 'block' and stop listening when they encounter a word they don't know. To break them of this habit, give them a 'numbers dictation' in which they must only write down the numbers they hear.

   We left home at ten o'clock. We travelled in two cars – three of us in my car and four in Diane's . . .

4 *No good at listening? (2)*

   Preparation always makes listening easier. Use pictures of the situation and speakers. Discuss the topic and introduce key vocabulary. Ask the students what they would expect to hear in this situation. Prediction work is very useful.

5 *No good at listening? (3)*

   Students need time to adjust to strange voices so let them hear the whole recording before you begin to ask questions.

6 *Let the students make recordings*

   Let the students write and record a dialogue in a specific situation – a post office, railway station, shop etc. and then ask them to prepare comprehension questions so that you can use the recording with another class. Jokes and anecdotes are also useful.

7 *Grade the task and not the text!*

   Students can handle quite difficult materials recorded from the TV or radio provided that you give plenty of preparation and move gradually from very simple questions to more difficult ones.

8 *Listen and read*

Give the students a reading passage and then let them listen to a recording in which the information is slightly different. Ask them to find the differences.

9 *Listen to songs*

Songs with comprehensible lyrics make good listening materials. Ask them to fill in the missing words in the text:

Strangers in the _____

Exchanging _____

Stangers in the _____

Know what _____ is

Or choose a song which tells a story and use it as a normal listening text.

10 *Before you finish*

Try to let the students see a printed version of the listening text or let them help you write it on the board if it is not too long. This exercise will reveal to you and to the students the difference between what they think they heard and what was actually said.

Speaking

1 *Oral practice and Oral fluency*

In *Oral practice* (drills, paired practice, etc.) students are expected to use a controlled and limited number of language patterns repeatedly. During oral practice students are learning the language they need to become fluent.

Oral fluency activities (project work, problem solving, role play, etc.) utilise a wide range of language and focus on communication rather than grammatical perfection. The aim is to develop confidence and to allow the students to use the language they have studied.

2 *Activity focus – Accuracy or fluency?*

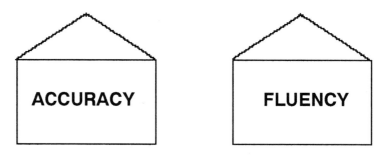

ACCURACY

FLUENCY

Let the students know if your focus is on accuracy or fluency. Make a card with 'Accuracy' on one side and 'Fluency' on the other. Use it to remind the students of the focus of their activity.

3

Student A

NAME	Mary	Tim	Sue	Tom
AGE	16	_____	12	_____
HOME	_____	Paris	_____	Rome
FOOD	Soup	_____	Cheese	_____

Student B

NAME	Mary	Tim	Sue	Tom
AGE	_____	11	_____	13
HOME	Oslo	_	Athens	_____
FOOD	_____	Toast	_____	Fruit

One of these cards is given to each student in a pair. Each student must try to complete the card by asking questions. The cards create an 'information gap'. These cards practise 'How old is _____?', 'Where does _____ live?', 'What does _____ like?'

(For more materials like this see the Longman series *Meridian Plus* by Jeremy Harmer)

4   *Find someone who . . .*

Find someone who can whistle.

Find someone who can play the guitar.

Find someone who can ride a horse.

Find someone who can write with their left hand.

Cards like this are used to practise one structure ('can' in this case) or a range of structures. Students move around the room asking questions and writing the names of people who fit the requirements.

5   *Similarities and Differences*

What are the similarities and differences between a dog and a cat?
Dogs have four legs and so do cats.
Dogs can't climb trees but cats can.
Dogs wag their tails when they're happy. Cats wag their tails when they're angry.

This task can integrate discussion with written practice as students, in pairs, discuss similarities and differences and make notes.

6   *Talking about talking*

Who said these things?
Where did they say them?
Who were they speaking to?
Why did they say them?

'Just one lump, please.'
'May I have your attention, please?'
'They've eaten it!'
'Are socks on this floor?'

This is great fun and encourages students to use their knowledge and imagination. Ask them to listen for more strange phrases to try on the class.

Reading

1   *Read what?*

Students on a holiday course in an English speaking community are surrounded by reading material. Don't limit them to books! Let them read posters, warning signs, bottles, packets, tickets, timetables, advertisements, magazines, catalogues, washing instructions, maps, newspapers, menus, guide books, etc.

2   *Spiral comprehension*

Start from the general and move to the specific as described on the 'Listening' page.

3 *Comprehension questions*

Yes/No questions are easy because the students don't need to compose a reply. Multiple choice questions are a little more difficult. 'Wh' questions are more challenging.
Always ask the students to support their answers by reference to the text.

4 *Corrupted reading is fun!*

Students enjoy reading corrupted texts.
You can _____ out words.
You can add and extra words.
Youcanjoinwordstogether.
Youca nspli tword sinto equal group slike this.
You can lav out lttrs.

It's a game and a valuable learning activity.

5 *Jigsaw*

Make several copies of the same text. Cut it into different sections with scissors. Let groups of students try to reconstruct the text.

6 *Read for content and style*

When you have studied a text ask the students:
Who was it written for?
Who wrote it?
Where does it come from? – newspaper, novel, magazine etc.
Why was it written?
Which aspects of the style help you to answer these questions?

7 *Read fast, Read often, Read well*

Students usually know only one style of reading. Start at the top left of the passage and then read down, word by word, line by line, until you reach the bottom right.
Teach your students to read quickly!

1 Look at title, headlines and any pictures. What is the passage about?
2 Read any sub-headings. What is the passage about?
3 Read the first sentence of each paragraph. What is the passage about?
4 Read the whole passage. What is the passage about?
   GIVE TIME LIMITS FOR EACH STEP!

Many of the activities which take place during the skills development lessons should be linked to other events during the course. Once you begin thinking in this way, you will not find it difficult to come up with ideas. One of the benefits will be seen in the students' vocabulary development. The close integration of language work with other activities will mean that students will gain greater language benefit from sports, excursions, meals and cultural activities.

For reading practice you will also be able to exploit newspapers and magazines. The radio and television can be excellent sources of topical listening material.

Try to go beyond the typical carefully graded reading and listening materials found in coursebooks. Let them use this opportunity to attempt to understand unprocessed authentic materials. Read Christine Nuttall's book *Teaching Reading Skills in a Foreign Language* and train the students to confront authentic texts which interest them.

The students will probably not be taught by native speakers of English in their normal school classes so let them take advantage of their holiday course by developing their pronunciation. You are a native speaker model so encourage them to copy your pronunciation. Choral speaking of poems or even the lyrics of pop songs can be an enjoyable and valuable activity.

Writing

1   *Write what?*

Stories, Exercises, Letters, Postcards, Advertisements, Notes, Posters, Captions to pictures, Maps, Poems, Songs, Jokes, Essays, Summaries, Lists, etc.

2   *Write where?*

Exercise books, Board, Wall Newspaper, Project displays, crosswords, scrapbook diary, letters, postcards, posters, T-shirt, skin (with washable ink), etc.

3   *Written practice and written fluency*

Be sure that you know the difference between the two – look at the relevant section on the 'Speaking' page.

4   *Writing in groups*

Writing does not need to be an individual activity. Group writing develops both oral and written fluency because the group argue about what to write and how they should write it! Start with pairs or groups of students doing a written exercise before moving on to more creative work.

5   *Learning to correct and edit written work*

Make photocopies of a student's written work and distribute them to the class. Let them read through the text and note their own ideas for changes or corrections. Then work through the text with the whole class to produce a corrected version on the board. After doing this encourage students to ask their class mates to correct and edit their written work.

6   *Make your writing more exciting!*

A man went into a bank. He had a gun. He asked for some money. He put the money in his bag. He went out of the bank.

A tall, dark-haired man dashed into a large, important bank. He pointed an ugly-looking, machine gun at a frightened clerk and demanded £10 000. With quivering fingers, the clerk collected the crisp bundles of £50 notes. The thief thrust the bundles into an old leather bag and rushed out of the bank.

Building a story in this way can be a class activity at first, but later it can be done in groups.

7   *Early steps to connected writing*

Labelling diagrams, Writing captions to pictures, Adding speech bubbles to pictures, Making posters, Filling forms, Answering questionnaires, Completing letters, etc.

8   *Plan carefully, Write quickly, Write well!*

Most students try to write the final version at the first attempt. They write slowly, get bored by what they are writing and quickly lose the thread of their argument. Good writing comes from planning, drafting and editing *before* you start the final version.

Step one – Collect your ideas

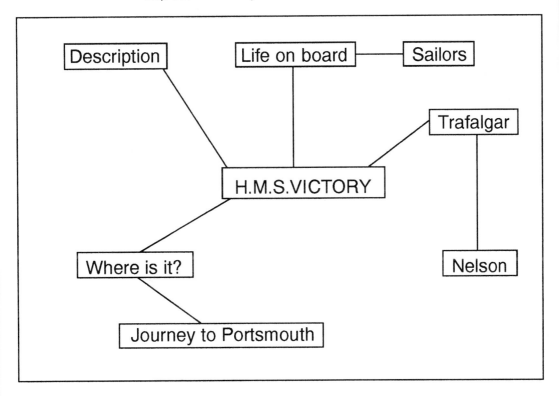

Step two – Organise in paragraphs
1   Journey to Portsmouth
2   Description H.M.S. Victory
3   Nelson and Trafalgar
4   Life of sailors on board

Step three – First draft

Step four – Read, compare, correct, edit
Students can get help from their colleagues or the teacher at this stage.

Step five – final version

5.8
Project work

Project work gives students the opportunity to use their knowledge of English to do research and present their results. When the students are at home, their local schools do not often find the time or facilities to allow the students to do project work in a foreign language. The relaxed atmosphere of a holiday course is a perfect opportunity to pursue this type of work.

Projects may be done by individual students but are more commonly done by students working in groups. The idea is for them to do research and then collect their ideas into some form of presentation. This may be a project book, a wall display, a sound (or video) recording or a dramatic presentation. On a holiday course popular topics will exploit the local area such as the follwoing:

1   The history of a local church or monument
2   The range of different places of worship in the area and the numbers of regular worshippers
3   How prices of common foods vary in local shops and supermarkets
4   The relative popularity of different national newspapers in the area
5   The services offered by the post office
6   Comparison of prices of different ways of travelling to London from the local town
7   The life of a famous local person
8   Local television preferences
9   How the local town makes its money
10 Local agriculture or industry

Many of these topics will involve the students in doing surveys. If they are going to collect information from shop keepers or other members they will have to be taught how to ask for information politely. Producing a questionnaire is a very subtle linguistic operation, particularly if it is to have multiple choice responses. The language work connected with preparing the questions, collecting and collating the data, and then recording it in some form of presentation will involve the exploitation of a very wide range of linguistic skills.

Try to avoid flooding the local town with students stopping the local people to ask questions. Don't allow the students to ask excessively personal questions:-

Do you believe in God?
How much do you earn?
How did you vote in the last election?
When did you last have a bath?

but most other topics would be suitable for some kind of research. The students may also be able to make use of the local public library or the library in the school you are occupying.

Even students with very little language ability can do simple projects. They might, for example, produce a project book on one of their class mates, in which they write and illustrate their friends' lives. This type of project would have even more language value if they were to do the same type of project on one of the children in their host family.

Outside the classroom

1   *In town*

Prepare worksheets for the students and see who can complete the sheet first.

Sample Questions

When was St Peter's Church built?

How many cans of Fanta can you buy for £3 at Tesco?

How much is a spring roll at the Bamboo House?

Whose statue stands in the square? Why was he famous?

Can you change foreign currency at the Post Office?

How much does it cost to send a postcard to Japan?

You could also give them a map with various places marked and ask the students to find the names of these places.

2   *Vocabulary and cars*

Do your students know the names of the different parts of a car – steering wheel, brake, clutch, etc? A lesson in the car park can introduce all this vocabulary. Consider different colours, ages, makes, models. Think of movement – going faster, slowing down, turning left, etc. What are the controls used for?

The brake is used to stop the car.

3   *In the countryside*

What happens in different seasons? What are the names of the different crops on the farm and their uses? What is an ecological chain? Who eats what? What is the life cycle of different animals, birds and insects?

4   *At the railway station*

Railway stations are full of displays of pictorial and printed information. Why not use these for reading comprehension? Listen to the station announcements for authentic listening comprehension.

5   *Pretend to be a tourist guide*

By the second or third week of a course the students should know the town quite well. As you walk the students through the town, ask them one at a time to pretend to be a tourist guide and point out the interesting places and tell the group about them. This activity can be even better if the students have had some time to prepare and each talks about a specific building or area.

6   *Organisation and discipline*

Always discuss your plans for going outside the school premises with the DOS. Try to keep your class together but avoid blocking the pavements in busy areas.

As an alternative (or sometimes in addition) to project work some schools organise a wall newspaper. This takes the form of a large notice board divided into sections like a normal newspaper. It contains feature articles, reports, reviews, cartoons, jokes, advertisements, drawings and photographs produced by the students. On a holiday course you can usually produce a weekly wall newspaper with all the classes making contributions. The most positive aspect of this type of work is that the students' work is put on display and can be read by all the other students in the school.

5.9
Scrap book diary

I have said that the job of a holiday course is to produce memories for the students. You can help this process by getting the students to produce souvenirs of their holiday course. A diary has an enormous power to stimulate the memory and when it is illustrated with photographs, drawings, bus tickets, menus, extracts from guide books, and postcards it becomes a wonderful record of a holiday course.

The amount of writing in the diary will vary from student to student. At the lowest levels it may be just a list of the day's activities but more advanced students can write more detailed accounts of their impressions and experiences. There is no reason why every student should not produce a personal scrap book diary.

In order to create this type of scrap book diary, students will need little more than a plain scrap book, some paper, sticky tape and encouragement. Some students will claim that they can't think of anything to write. In this case it is up to the teacher to make suggestions. Even something as banal as describing and commenting on a meal would be useful.

If you are concerned that students may take home a diary full of uncorrected grammatical errors, you should ask the students to prepare their diary entries on paper so that when the final corrected version is produced, this is stuck into the diary.

The resulting diaries will not only make useful records for the students when they leave but will also give their parents some idea of what they have done during the course.

5.10
Organisation of students' files

Many holiday course organisations give their students files in which to keep all the handouts from their lessons and their own written work. If this is the practice at the holiday course where you are working, you will have to train the students to organise these files so that they can make quick reference to material in the file.

It is preferable if all the students use the same filing system. This can be:

(a) chronological – putting the date on each item and then filing by date.

(b) by topic – so all materials relating to 'grammar' are stored together, etc.

(c) by teacher – so all the materials given by, or done for a particular teacher are stored together.

It is a good idea if the scrapbook diary and the vocabulary notebook are kept separately from the rest of the materials.

SECTION C

THE LEISURE PROGRAMME

I wish that there was a less pejorative title for this part of the programme of holiday courses. 'Leisure Programme' suggests that these activities are in some way less important than the language programme. This is not the case. The value of a holiday course must be judged in terms of overall development and maturity rather than just language learning. A holiday course which did not have an organised leisure programme would be much less beneficial to the students.

6

Excursions

**6.0
Responsibility
for excursions**

Many holiday courses appoint an Excursions Director to be responsible for the organising of excursions. Others appoint a Social Director to be responsible for excursions, sports and social activities. Sometimes the Course Director has overall responsibility for coordinating excursions, but the basic organisation of each excursion is delegated to individual members of staff.

The organiser of the excursions will call upon other members of staff to assist in publicity and supervision of groups of students during the outing. Language teachers will want to exploit the excursions for their language potential.

This chapter is addressed both to those readers who will be organising excursions and those who will merely assist on supervision. Excursions offer a potential for problems which are different from those encountered in the average classroom or gymnasium, so it is useful to be prepared!

**6.1
Three types of
excursion**

There are essentially three types of excursion: cultural excursions, pleasure visits and shopping trips. All three can be valuable and memorable experiences for the students provided that the staff plan and prepare the excursions with care. Each has a different purpose and each requires a different kind of preparation.

<table>
<tr><td>6.1.1
Duration and
Timing</td><td>Excursions usually last for a full day if a long journey is involved. Students may be taken to nearer destinations for a morning or afternoon. Many schools take the students on full day excursions at weekends which has various disadvantages. On Saturdays and Sundays, many students will either arrive or leave for home so several teachers may be involved in airport transfers. At weekends road traffic is often heavier and slower moving than on weekdays. Popular sites for outings are extremely crowded and students may have to wait for an hour or more for admission. The large crowds also makes it more difficult to see what there is to be seen. On Sundays most shops are closed and this can turn an interesting city into a lifeless collection of old buildings. Cathedrals and other churches have a heavy programme of religious services and do not encourage large groups of sightseers.</td></tr>
</table>

There are many good reasons for selecting a weekday for full day excursions. The teaching week of lessons is broken into two shorter periods allowing better opportunities for preparation before the excursion and follow up afterwards. Having two and three day teaching periods may also make it easier to move students who have been assigned to classes at the wrong level. Students who are leaving on a Saturday or Sunday do not feel that they are unfairly missing one of the excursions. Midweek excursions will mean that lessons are also given on Saturday but students are unlikely to object to this.

6.2
Cultural
Excursions

Cultural excursions are often to sites of historical or cultural interest; castles, country houses, art galleries, museums and so on. Since each visit will tend to focus on a particular period in history or series of events, the preparation for the excursion should attempt to put that period into its historical context. In this way the teacher will make the excursions as enjoyable and valuable as possible.

6.2.1
Selecting
destinations for
cultural excursions

The success of a cultural visit rests partly on the selection of the destination. The criteria for selecting a site include its cultural significance, the age and interests of the students, the length of the journey, the convenience and cost.

The first factor to consider is the age of the group of students. Visits to the Stock Exchange may be very popular with some adult students but would be a total waste of time for younger students. When considering the cultural aspects of an excursion, you should not think of the inherent value of the place but the benefit which the students are likely to get from the visit. A group of children will get more benefit from a trip to a farm or a model village than a tour around Westminster Abbey.

The best choices will have an immediate visual appeal to the students so castles and cathedrals are usually better than museums or art galleries. If the students already know some of the history connected with a place, they will be more likely to appreciate the visit. They will be more interested in things which move than static buildings. They will be even more excited by places where they can be active. Perhaps you can organise a visit to a pottery where the students can make things with clay. Visits to factories where students can see machines and craftsmen at work can be enjoyable and memorable. I have known schools who organised short visits to the local supermarket in which the local manager was prepared to talk about how the shop was laid out, organised and run.

A valuable cultural visit can be ruined by the absence of a good snack bar or a long wait for the toilets. Similarly, a long, boring coach journey can spoil the effect of the most exciting destination.

6.2.2
Planning a
cultural excursion

As an example let's consider the planning of a visit to HMS *Victory* in Portsmouth. We mentioned in Chapter 1 that the job of the holiday course was to feed memories. If we do no planning or preparation, the students will only remember going to see an old wooden ship. None of the history associated with that ship will be absorbed and the excursion will be wasted. How might we change this situation?

The procedure might be as follows: When planning the excursion programme each teacher or group leader is asked to be responsible for preparation for one excursion. Three or four weeks before the planned date of the excursion the teacher goes to the planned destination (in our example HMS *Victory*). The teacher tours the site in exactly the same way as the group of students will do. The teacher takes photographs (preferably slides) while on tour and perhaps records the comments of the guide if there is one. The teacher buys the guidebooks and learns about the history of the place. The teacher's observations are not limited to the cultural aspects of the tour. The teacher also looks at the siting of toilets, the coach park, the restaurant, the souvenir shop and any suitable areas where a group of students might eat a packed lunch.

Using the materials collected on the preliminary visit, the teacher creates an illustrated presentation about the excursion. The teacher will probably prepare a questionnaire or worksheet which the students can complete whilst on the trip.

About a week before the excursion the teacher will produce a poster advertising the excursion and the illustrated presentation which will be given the evening before. The purpose of this presentation is to inform the students BEFORE they go on the excursion so that when they see the actual site, it reminds them of what they have already seen in the presentation.

The presentation, which should last no more than about half an hour, explains the historical background to the most important things which the students will see. Placing events into a historical context is more difficult than it may seem at first sight. When working with foreign students we cannot assume an understanding of (British) history. Although the visit may focus on political events, it will be easier to arouse the students' interest in the social conditions of the time. The development of social history will produce more parallels with the history of their own countries which the students learn at school. They will also find it easier to identify with a 'powder monkey' in HMS *Victory* than with Horatio Nelson.

An Excursion Poster

Wednesday 13th July

Excursion to HMS VICTORY – the most famous battleship in Britain.

Join the coaches outside the school at 9am.

Return to school at about 7pm.

H.M.S. VICTORY

A YOUNG PERSON'S VISIT RECORD

What to look for on the Ship

- Can you see the Admiral's flag at the top of the Mainmast? When it is flying, it shows that the Admiral is on active duty | Yes | No |

- Did you see the Union Flag (the Jack) flying on the staff? | |

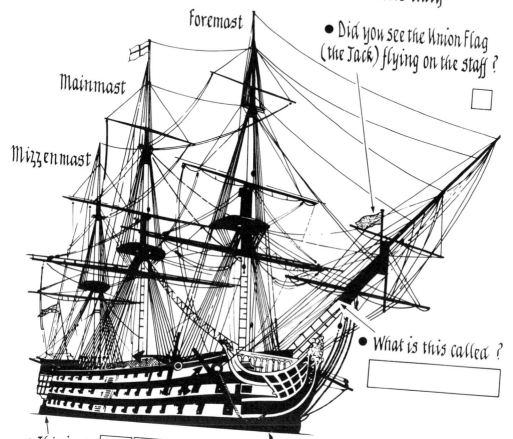

Foremast

Mainmast

Mizzenmast

- What is this called?

  | |

- This is the | Bow | Stern | of the ship
- The front is called the | Bow | Stern |
- On how many decks can you see guns? 1 2 or 3

Dimensions

- ⚓ Overall length 328 feet (99·97 metres)
- ⚓ Length of hull 226 feet (68·88 metres)
- ⚓ Height of Main Mast from the Quarter Deck 165·5 feet (50·5 metres)
- ⚓ Overall width 51·83 feet (15·8 metres)
- ⚓ Tonnage 2162 tons

Excursion Worksheet

1 Which town is HMS *Victory* in?

2 What does HMS stand for?

3 What is the front of a ship called, the bow or the stern?

4 If you stand on deck facing the bow of the ship, the port side is on your left and the starboard side is on your right. Where did you enter the ship, on the port side or starboard side?

5 The different floors of a ship are called decks. How many different decks are there on HMS *Victory*?

6 How many decks have guns on them?

7 On which deck was Nelson standing when he was fatally wounded?

8 Which arm had Nelson lost?

9 Nelson was 'Admiral of the Fleet', who was the captain of HMS *Victory* at the Battle of Trafalgar?

10 What is a cat o' nine tails and what was it used for?

11 Where is Trafalgar?

12 Who were the British fighting against at the Battle of Trafalgar?

13 The Battle of Trafalgar was on 21st October of which year?

14 Where is Nelson's body buried?

15 Where and when was HMS *Victory* built?

16 Where did the wood come from?

17 Where did the ordinary sailors sleep?

18 What did they eat?

19 How many men lived on the lower gun deck?

20 What did the powder monkeys do?

In the case of our visit to HMS *Victory*, the aims of the presentation would be to teach the following information:

(a) the battle of Trafalgar in 1805 was part of many years of war between France and Britain.

(b) HMS *Victory* was one of the ships which took part in the battle. It was commanded by Admiral Nelson who was in charge of the whole fleet of British ships.

(c) Admiral Nelson is the man standing on the top of the column in Trafalgar Square in London.

(d) Admiral Nelson had already fought many battles against the French and had lost an eye and an arm in the process.

(e) Although Admiral Nelson was killed in the battle, it was still considered a great British victory.

As you will see the aims of the presentation are very limited. Social history might be left to the questionnaire or worksheet which students would be given to complete during the visit. The questionnaire should contain questions which can be answered through looking at things: 'What colour is . . .?', 'How many . . .?' and some questions which can be answered through understanding language: 'What was the name given to the boys who carried gunpowder to the guns?' 'How did people become sailors in the navy?' These questionnaires can be used as the basis for follow up work in language classes after the excursion.

6.2.3
Exploiting the
excursion

You want the students to remember the excursion for as long as possible. Encourage them to use their cameras to take photographs. You might organise a competition for the best drawing of HMS *Victory*. Give them time to buy souvenirs and guidebooks. Encourage them to buy postcards. In the language class, they can write about the excursion. Don't get excessively excited about the *culture* aspect of the trip. If a student's first reaction to the HMS *Victory* visit is to think about what life would be like with only one arm, then you should not feel that the excursion has been wasted. The other reactions are present but they may take more time to surface.

6.2.4
Where shall I
take them?

An Excursions Director needs good contact with the local tourist information centre. Here you will be able to get calendars of local events, leaflets describing historic monuments, theme parks, zoos, carnivals and so on. More importantly, if you are a stranger to the area, the local tourist information centre will give you advice on which items might be suitable for your students.

6.3
Pleasure visits

Although you may think there is no obvious cultural value in taking students to a funfair, regatta, highland games, gymkhana, scramble, stock car races, dog races or a horse race meeting, these excursions are not a waste of time. A local village fair or church fete will offer stalls, tombolas, side shows (guess the weight of the cake, fortune tellers, coconut shys, etc.) and usually some entertainment. All these can be seen as cultural visits to present day Britain. Students will be in close proximity to the British at play. The students will see and hear a great deal which can be a stimulus for some very interesting language work. The students can certainly talk and write about their own activities during the visit but they can also be encouraged to discuss and record the way that other people behaved. Were all the people dressed in the same way? How did people react at the end of a race? Did the people who had won react in the same way as the people who lost? How would people react in your own country in the same situation? This type of observation should not be used simply to highlight differences between British behaviour and that in the students' own countries. We should also try to focus on similarities.

An excursion to an ice skating rink, a bowling alley, a pop concert or disco can be a popular and successful social event. In these cases, always tell the proprietors that you want to bring a certain number of students. It can be very frustrating to arrive and to be refused entry. Students may also enjoy a country (or city) walk or a 'fun run'. When teaching adult students these excursions may become a cultural pub crawl.

**6.4
Shopping trips**

These excursions will benefit from language presentation. Teaching useful phrases for shopping has immediate relevance and value if it precedes a shopping expedition. Discuss with the students the things that they would like to buy. Discuss and elicit the type of language which would be useful. 'Have you got it in a bigger/smaller size?' 'I'm not too keen on this colour, have you got any different colours?' 'How much does it cost?' 'Have you got any cheaper ones?', etc. Role play the scene in the shop, first by taking the part of the shop assistant yourself. Then get one of the students to play the shop assistant. In a follow-up lesson you might get the students to bring the things they bought to the lesson. You can discuss the items and the transactions which took place. This type of work makes the students feel that the lessons are really worthwhile.

6.4.1
Shop-lifting

A shopping trip provides a useful opportunity to remind the students of the consequences of shop-lifting. Some students who feel that they have escaped from parental control try to demonstrate their bravery by stealing from shops. Shops are increasingly keen to proceed with police prosecution of shop-lifters. You should tell the students that even if there is no prosecution, the offenders will certainly be sent home immediately and their parents will be informed of the offence.

**6.5
Discipline on
excursions**
6.5.1
Supervision

Excursions need to be supervised in order to support the students and maintain discipline. The correct ratio of adult supervisors to students depends on the age of the students. We do not want the students to feel that their freedom is being excessively restricted but they should realise that foreign students are often seen as easy targets for petty thieves and others.

If students are to be given 'free' time to wander around, it is best to put limits on their wandering area. 'As far as the end of this street but no further.'

It is very important that you should know all the students in your group and that you have an accurate list of their names. With young students, it is useful to be able to describe the missing child. Descriptions of height, clothing, hair colour and length are more useful for spotting a child in a crowd than passport photographs, colour of eyes and 'mole on left elbow'! Why not make the students responsible for remembering what another student is wearing on the excursion. This could even be a game on the coach.

We all have fears of losing students when they are on excursions. Every student should be equipped with a card giving their full name and the name and address of the school (and their host family if they have one). The card should also contain an emergency telephone number to use if they get lost. The students should be informed of what they should do if they get separated from the rest of the party. You will find it useful if you wear distinctive clothing (I know of one language school where the teachers are all provided with bright red sweat shirts). If you are tall a distinctive hat will make you easy to spot at a distance. Remember to count your group regularly and identify those students who have a tendency to stray.

6.5.2
Coach journeys

If you are using a coach, make sure that the students get a good look at the outside of the coach so that they can identify it at a distance. Have a large card with the name of the school which you can put in the front window of the coach so that students can check that they are getting in the correct coach. In Britain it is traditional to have a collection for the coach driver on the return journey (provided he has been helpful and pleasant). It is up to you whether you maintain this tradition with your students. However, I would seriously suggest that you arrange for the driver to receive some form of tip. The drivers have to put up with a lot of noise and hassle in their work and a little extra financial reward helps to keep up a good relationship with the coach firm. If you can encourage your students to say a polite 'Thank you very much' to the driver as they leave the coach, then so much the better.

If the coach journey is going to be quite long, you will have to make arrangements to stop so that the students can use the toilet. They are certain to have over-indulged in soft drinks during the outing. You should be very careful about discipline on the coach. If you teach the students some of the travelling games (collecting names of pubs, doing the alphabet with car numbers etc.) this will help to amuse the students during the coach journey. Try to keep down the level of noise. It is hard enough to drive a large, long coach without the distraction of 52 students shouting at each other in 20 different languages.

Every summer we hear of accidents involving coach parties with horrifying deaths and injuries. Coaches are not yet fitted with seat belts but you should realise that the dangers associated with a sudden stop are just as great in a coach as in a car. For this reason you should try to make sure that the students remain seated while the coach is moving. It would also be sensible if you followed the same rule.

Many students get travel sick on long coach journeys. Try to identify those students before you start and ask them if they normally take a travel sickness pill. If so try to make sure they take one before the journey.

Checklist for Coach Journeys

1 Before you get on the coach

(a) Check that you have a kitchen roll, some water and paper cups and some sickness bags to deal with travel sick students. You will also need a large plastic bag for litter on the coach.

(b) Check that you know where you are going and where, if at all, the other coaches plan to stop for drinks, toilets, etc. on the way.

(c) Check that all the students have used the toilet before they start the journey. Also check that those students who are regularly travel sick have taken their travel sickness pills.

(d) Check that you know the telephone number of the school so that you can inform the Course Director if the coach breaks down or becomes seriously delayed by traffic during the journey.

(e) Check that students have remembered to bring the things they will need during the excursion – cameras, walkmen, worksheets, pencils, packed lunches, etc. (Students will need their watches if they are to be at a fixed place at a certain time.)

(f) Check that you have a sign board giving the name of the school to put in the front window of the coach.

(g) Draw the students' attention to the outside of the coach. They will need to identify it later.

(h) If you are going to need money for entrance tickets, food, tip for the driver, etc., check that you have enough.

2 Before you leave the school

(a) Count all the students on the coach. Have any been left behind?

(b) Have any supervisors been left behind?

(c) Greet the coach driver and find out her/his name and give your own.

3 During the journey

(a) Tell the students to remain seated and keep them as quiet as possible.

(b) Tell the students to look at the clothing which their friends are wearing and remember it.

4 When you arrive

(a) Tell the students if they have to stick together or if they are free to wander. In the latter case, tell them how far they can wander.

(b) Agree with the driver where and when the coach will collect the students.

(c) Tell the students what you have agreed with the driver.

(d) Tell the students that they must come back on the same coach!

(e) Remind the students of the dangers of pickpockets and tell them to be careful with their money and valuables.

(f) It may also be necessary to remind students about the consequences of stealing.

(g) Remind students that they are not allowed to feed the animals, touch the exhibits or get out of the coach in the lion enclosure!

(h) Tell the students where the nearest public toilets are situated.

5   **During the visit**

   (a) If you are leading a group of students try to have a distinctive hat or other item of clothing so that students can spot you from a distance. A brightly coloured umbrella can also be used.

   (b) Count and recount the students regularly and make sure they are your students and not those from another group or school.

   (c) Pay special attention to wandering students if you or the students need to wait in line for any length of time.

6   **Returning**

   (a) Check that students have used the toilet, taken travel sickness pills, bought postcards, etc. before you leave.

   (b) Check and double check that you have all the correct students.

   (c) Check with your colleagues on other coaches whether they plan to stop on the way back.

   (d) Apply the same rules about staying in seats as on the outward journey.

   (e) Make a 'collection for driver' if appropriate.

7   **Arriving back at school**

   (a) Remind students not to leave their personal belongings on the coach.

   (b) Make sure that the students thank the driver and do so yourself.

Activities on Coach Journeys

1 Worksheet

1 Why are some direction indication signs green and others blue?

2 Which is the oldest of these cars?
C941 TOP   POT 423C   POT 362
Which is the newest?

3 What is the speed limit in towns?

4 What is the speed limit on motorways?

5 Which has priority, a car on a roundabout or a car joining a roundabout?

6 What is the meaning of the big L which you see on some cars?

7 What is the meaning of double yellow lines beside the road?

8 What is the missing step in the normal sequence of traffic lights at a crossroads?
   1 **Red**
   2 **Red and yellow**
   3 **Green**
   4 _____

9 What are the **AA** and the **RAC**?

10 Approximately how fast is 50 miles per hour in kilometres per hour?

2 'Legs' cricket (in pairs)

Each player has eleven batsmen. Both players look for pub signs. The batting player looks for pub names which contain 'legs'. – 'The Red Lion' has four legs and gives four runs. 'The Duke of Gloucester' scores two runs. 'The Pig and Canary' scores six. A 'legless' pub, such as 'The King's Arms' or 'The Castle' causes a wicket to fall and the batsman is out.

3 Observation game (in pairs)

The students try to spot the following things from the coach and score points. A possible scoring system is shown below.

10 A car with a caravan
20 A milk float
30 A police car
40 An ambulance
50 A fire engine
60 A horse and cart

4 Observation game 2

If you see a police car, fire engine or ambulance, you must hold your collar until you see an 'H' registration car (or whatever is the latest letter).

Never encourage students to take medicines they are unsure about, but make sure that you have some sickness bags, tissues and cold water on the coach!

6.5.3
Train journeys

Occasionally you may find that a train journey is an economic alternative to the hire of a coach. Travelling by train adds a further aspect to the cultural value of an excursion. Students can do useful language work associated with trains by looking at all the printed notices that they see in the carriages and from the windows. They can be asked to record the time when the train stops at each station. Later they can check this against the published timetable to check on the punctuality of the train. It is also possible to do some lessons with small groups of students on the train.

Discipline on trains should be as good as it is on coaches. You may also need to remind the students that they should not disturb the other passengers.

7

Social and cultural activities

**7.0
Aims**

Students on holiday courses have been separated from their homes and families. The job of the holiday course organisation is to keep the students happy and this usually means keeping them busy. They will be busy for much of the day with language lessons, sports and having meals. If nothing has been organised for the wet afternoons and the evenings the students will tend to hang around in large or small groups on street corners or outside hamburger bars. Many of the students may be very happy to do this but it will not be appreciated by the local community. The unfortunate incidents when foreign students have been approached by drug pushers or have been sexually harassed have usually resulted from the lack of a social and cultural programme.

The aim of the programme is to give the students something to do, to encourage interaction between the students and perhaps also with the local community.

**7.1
Planning the
social and
cultural
programme**

There is a constant danger that the students will feel excessively regimented. Those that form new friendships quickly will often have no difficulty in filling their spare time. The social and cultural programme needs to consider the less gregarious students who need to be encouraged to participate. Thus the programme should include a balance of organised events involving all students and 'options' periods when there will be a choice of activities for the students. The selection of events and options will obviously depend on the number and ages of the students. In some large schools it may be better to have different social programmes for senior and junior students.

In order to administer the programme you need good sources of information for the students. A large, prominent, clearly presented notice board is essential. Like the sports notice board it should provide details of the programme for the next four or five days so it needs to be updated daily. The events on the social programme can also be promoted during lessons.

Social Programme Questionnaire

Please mark the circle beside the activities you enjoy

NAME . . . .

CLASS . . . .

Music
O Singing
O Playing the piano
O Playing the guitar
O Playing another instrument

      Please specify . . . .

Arts and crafts
O Painting and drawing
O Origami
O Brass rubbing
O Photography
O Printing T-shirts
O Candle making
O Jewellery making
O Model making
O Face painting
O Shell sculpture, stone painting
O Cooking
O Embroidery

Theatre
O Acting and mime
O Modern dancing
O Ballet

History
O Local history
O British history
O International history

Geography
O Local geography
O Geography of Britain
O Nature study

Media studies
O T.V. and radio
O Newspapers and magazines

Computer studies
O Computer games
O Computer Programming
O Word processing

Literature
O Poetry and verse
O Literature of this area
O History of literature

Entertainments
O Disco
O Video films
O Cinema
O Theatre
O Classical music Concerts
O Rock concerts
O Jazz concerts
O Cards and board games

Spectator sports
O Cricket
O Football
O Rugby
O American football
O Athletics
O Basketball
O Horse racing
O Dog racing
O Tennis
O Other sports
     Please specify

. . . .

. . . .

7.1.1 Events and options	As mentioned above the main difference between EVENTS and OPTIONS are the number of students involved. Many of the excursions will be events because all the students in the school will be involved. Other ideas for events are described below. Options are for smaller groups of students and are intended to cater for the minority interests. Some schools give students a questionnaire when they arrive listing all the possible options. The students mark those that interest them. After this the most requested options are included in the social programme. The notice board will list the available options each day and students are asked to sign up for their chosen options.
7.1.2 Social events	Social events will usually involve all the students as performers or spectators. They often require some degree of planning and preparation as will be seen in the ideas listed below. They are very useful in establishing a sense of group identity amongst the students which is important to the success of a holiday course.

7.1.3
Performances
	Some of the most successful holiday courses I know, prepare and perform a full musical in two or three weeks. All the students are involved as actors, singers, dancers, musicians, costume designers, scenery painters and so on. The performances are given for the host families and others from the local community. The preparation for the final performances acts as a focus for the holiday course. This obviously requries a lot of cooperative effort from the holiday course staff but all find the work both satisfying and rewarding. As you can imagine, the students greatly enjoy this collaboration and remember the experience for the rest of their lives. The benefit for students goes far beyond the new language they acquire.
	
	    The 'International Evening' is another form of entertainment which students can prepare. This is usually a combination of songs and dances performed by national groups and sketches written and performed by international groups. Once again, the performance is given for host families and other members of the local community.
	
	    The 'finals' of sporting events can also be popular spectator events. Sometimes the tensions of the rival teams and supporters can be relieved by staging a 'staff against students' match on the same evening.

7.1.4
Meals as events
	Many schools organise a barbecue as an alternative to the evening meal on one evening. This can be very popular particularly if you can organise songs around a 'camp fire' in the style of the scout movement. You could even consider inviting local troops of scouts or guides to join you for the barbecue. The young people will have plenty of experiences to share.
	
	    Some schools also organise 'formal' dinners. These give the students an opportunity to dress in their finest clothes and pretend to be lords and ladies for the evening. An alternative is to allow groups of students to prepare an evening meal. As I have mentioned in the chapter on meals, this will have to be negotiated carefully with the kitchen staff. These evenings of foreign food can often be very popular.
	
	    One way of combining a performance and a meal is to allow some groups of students to organise a cabaret after the meal. If you do this, try

to make sure that you can clear away all the plates, glasses, and eating utensils so that you do not delay the catering staff.

7.1.5 Lectures, slide shows or debates	In the chapter on Excursions I have mentioned that the cultural preparation could take the form of a lecture and slide show done by one of the teachers. Remember that you can also use the resources of the local community. Perhaps the local history society will send a speaker with a set of slides to talk about the local area. The local police are often willing to send someone to speak to the students. You will also find potential speakers amongst the school staff. Debates between students can also be lively social events provided that they can be kept under reasonable control. You will have to think carefully about the interests and the language levels of the students if you are going to make these lectures main events for all the students. Some may be more suitable as 'options' for smaller groups.
7.1.6 Films and videos	It may well be possible to hire films or videos locally and these can make popular communal entertainments for the students. There are legal restrictions on showing some videos to large audiences and you will have to be careful to choose suitable films. Students who have seen a film in their own language will often be very happy to see it again in the original language so don't reject old, but popular films.
7.1.7 Discos	The evening disco in the school is a regular and popular event at holiday courses. You will have to review the facilities and equipment available in the school but even the best equipped schools often choose to use an outside firm to provide music, sound systems and lights. An ordinary disco can be made special and memorable by having a theme. This may be musical like 'the sixties' or 'the seventies' or it could require costumes. 'Tramps' is a good theme because the costumes are simple. Similarly, 'Pyjama Parties' can be very amusing. Depending on the group and the opportunities for making costumes, you can decide on suitable themes. During a disco it is a good idea to have a few competitions. Students enjoy miming to the latest pop records so imitation competitions of their favourite pop stars are always popular. You will find students who would like to take part in disco dancing competitions. There may also be prizes for the best costume, 'the ugliest monster' and so on. Discos provide excellent opportunities for awarding prizes won in other activities. If you award the tennis prize at the disco it makes both events memorable. You should try to award as many prizes as you can and make sure that each winner is photographed receiving the prize from the course director. As I mention in the chapter on sports, the prizes can be certificates, medals or small cups.
7.1.8 Crazy games	A popular social event for a warm summer evening can be a gala of crazy games. These can range from the traditional bobbing for apples and passing oranges held under the chin to the elaborate obstacle races featured on 'It's a Knockout' or 'Jeux Sans Frontières'. The games may also have an educational value – I have occasionally included competitive bed making with marks for speed and style!

THURSDAY

1. DESIGN YOUR OWN T-SHIRT

Meet Alison in the artroom at 3.p.m. £5 for T-Shirt and materials. Bring your ideas!

2. Sherlock Holmes in Portsmouth

Learn about Sherlock Holmes - the world's most famous detective. Walk with Colin and see the house where A. Conan Doyle wrote the first Sherlock Holmes story! Meet Colin in Room A2 at 3·00p.m

3. SCOTTISH BARBECUE AT 7·00

McDougal's Hamburgers and Scotch Eggs with baked potatoes and Salad. Come and see Jimmy wearing his kilt! Come and taste a real Scottish Haggis! Jimmy will teach you Scottish dancing

4. Video - T.V. Room 8·30

"OLIVER" - A musical based on 'Oliver Twist' by Portsmouth-born author — Charles Dickens

FRIDAY

1. Murder in Portsmouth

Meet Alan in Room A2 at 3 o'clock. Visit the old city of Portsmouth and see the places where famous MURDERS took place!! Bring your camera and good walking shoes.

2. ROSIE'S MUSIC GROUP

3 p.m. in the Music Room. Today — American Musicals. Bring your voices even if you think you can't sing!!

3. TABLE TENNIS FINALS.

Giorgio Vs Kurt
7.30 p.m in the Games room. Come and cheer your heroes.

8.00 p.m. Gymnasium

4. Final Rehearsal

Sharon's Dance Display Group. Last chance to practise before tomorrow's disco!!

5. Video-T.V. Room 8.00

"THE SWARM" - Killer bees attack an American town !!

SATURDAY

"TRAMPS DISCO"

7.30 p.m in the Gymnasium
(Please wear soft shoes)

PRIZES FOR :-

BEST FEMALE COSTUME

BEST MALE COSTUME

* MIMING COMPETITION *

Michael Jackson's "Bad" Six prizes must be won !!
Dance Display - Sharon's Dance Display Group have prepared a special show for the Tramps Disco with music from Bananarama, Terence Trent Darby and Bros.

7.2
Options

The range of options which you can offer will depend on your imagination, and the skills and interests of the teaching staff and group leaders. It is a great mistake to imagine that teenagers are only interested in listening to pop music or playing with video games, the most obscure options from embroidery to bird watching can be very successful if presented with enthusiasm. In order to make up your options questionnaire you will have to find out the interests of the teaching staff and group leaders. You will find a curious range of talents! You will also have to review the options which are possible in the school or offered by the local area. Remember at all times the added value of these local options which often bring the students in to contact with local people.

The leaders of the option groups may be members of the teaching staff, group leaders or local people. The requirements of the leader are some knowledge and skill in the chosen topic and boundless enthusiasm. More importantly they must have the ability to transmit this enthusiasm to the students. The leaders do not need to be language experts and in some ways it is often an advantage if they are not. Language teachers invariably develop a specialised style of speech for students which is different from the speech of the general public.

Some of the options suggested below are linked to school subjects. This is not a disadvantage as all the students will be able to bring some knowledge to the group. However, the leaders should not be tempted to give traditional 'lessons' in the topic. The style throughout should encourage investigation and discovery.

7.2.1
Arts and crafts

Students can gain hours of pleasure from the pursuit of artistic endeavours. These may range from sketching and painting to brass rubbing or basket work. Some other crafts which might be considered are origami, candle making, simple jewellery making, shell sculpture, face painting, model aircraft construction and so on.

Many students will have cameras and some training in the skills and techniques of photography would be possible. Supa Snaps, the photographic chain, produce a cheap and attractively illustrated booklet, 'The Compact 35 mm Handbook' which explains clearly and simply the techniques of successful photography, composition, etc. This option could be linked to a photographic exhibition and competition for the students.

Needlework may seem old fashioned and unappealing to many students but learning to design and print their own T-shirts could be very popular.

A display of work done by former students (or photographs of that work) would be a good way to arouse the students' interest in some of the more unusual arts and crafts.

7.2.2
Music

Many students who attend holiday courses have some musical training. They would be happy to develop this and perhaps perform with other students. It might be possible to do some choral singing from the classical and popular repertoires. There are opportunities to take these skills outside the school premises. Could the group go to perform at a local hospital? Other outside activities include visits to local concerts. Would it be impossible to arrange a visit to a group of bell ringers in a local church?

7.2.3 History	An investigation of local history would offer a range of opportunities for optional activities. There may be potential for the study of industrial, social or political history. On a broader scale, students might want to investigate the history of relations between Britain and their own country.
7.2.4 Geography	Once again the potential of the local area will give the most immediate stimulus. Taking a broad view of geography, investigations could range from geology or wildlife to climate or transport systems. Some of these options can have links to other topic areas; wildlife might be linked to photography or sketching, transport systems to local history.
7.2.5 Media studies	Many students may not previously have considered this area of investigation so a visit to a foreign country would be a good opportunity to develop this interest. They might wish to concentrate their investigations in the area of newspapers, magazines, radio or television. They could make interesting comparisons with these media in their own countries.
7.2.6 Sports	The potential for sports options is vast. Some of these are considered in the chapter on sports.
7.3 Conclusions	In most holiday courses the variety of social and cultural activities is often very limited. So many opportunities are overlooked. Holiday course directors are always looking for elements which will make their courses different from the others but few have considered the development of cultural and educational options. The main aim of these activities is the enjoyment of the students but the reader will see that they will gain considerable language benefit because they will be using English all the time. The language programme will contribute to the cultural programme and vice versa.

8

Sports

**8.0
Aims**

Holiday courses usually offer a wide range of sporting activities to the students. These provide enjoyable relaxation from the language work and can serve to develop friendships between students of different nationalities. As we will see later, the students can also make contact with British people in circumstances which are not linguistically taxing.

The sporting activities on most holiday courses do not concentrate on sporting excellence. The aim is enjoyment which is achieved through variety, maximum participation, competition and the opportunity to learn something new.

There are many opportunities for language exploitation of sporting activities because the use of language is immediately connected with action. However most teachers feel that the language work should arise out of the needs of the situation rather than being artificially imposed on it.

**8.1
Planning**

The aims of the holiday course sports programme can be defined in three words placed in order of priority:- safety, variety and fun. These aims can only be achieved through careful preparation which will lead to a detailed, but flexible sports programme.

On some holiday courses the language teaching staff are also responsible for the organisation and execution of the sports programme. Increasingly, holiday course directors are recognising that this policy often puts excessive strain on the language teachers and leads to a reduction of standards in all fields. Now it is more frequent to find sports specialists working on holiday courses with one responsible for overall coordination.

When planning a sports programme for a holiday course the first thing to do is to review the numbers, qualifications and interests of the staff. The next step is to assess the range and condition of facilities available both within the school premises and in the local area. The sports staff will consider the age and likely interests of the students. The social director will look into the opportunities for activities which may be offered as alternatives to sports. Finally, the sports organiser and staff will plan for the days when wet weather makes outside sports impossible.

8.1.1
Preparing the programme

Most students stay on holiday courses for only two or three weeks so it should not be difficult to produce an imaginative programme even if the weather may be bad. Your aim should be to encourage the students to try as many different activities as possible.

The afternoon programme should offer a variety of activities each day. There will probably be a choice of traditional sports, specialist sports and other options.

Sports Questionnaire

Please mark the circle beside the sports you enjoy.

NAME ....

CLASS ....

Team games
o Football
o Rugby
o Lacrosse
o Hockey
o Basketball
o Netball
o Volleyball
o Rounders/Softball
o Water polo
o Croquet

Individual Activities
o Tennis
o Squash
o Badminton
o Gymnastics
o Swimming

o Diving
o Synchronised swimming
o Athletics
o Horse riding
o Cycling
o Ice skating
o Roller skating
o Skate board
o Archery
o Grass skiing
o Weight lifting
o Keep fit
o Aerobics
o Wind surfing
o Golf
o Rock climbing
o Table tennis
o Billiards
o Darts

Sports Notice board

MONDAY

1. AT THE SWIMMING POOL - MANDY

2·30 Swimming class - for non-swimmers
3·30 Under 13 Swimming
4·30 Over 13 Swimming

2. AT THE FOOTBALL FIELD - CHRIS

2·30 Over 13 football
4·00 Under 13 hockey

3. IN THE GYMNASIUM - SANDRA

2·30 Aerobics
3·30 Keep fit
4·30 Badminton

4. OTHER ACTIVITIES

2·30 Croquet - Neville (meet in A2)
2·30 Volleyball - Bill (meet front lawn)
2·30 Tennis - Paul (Tennis Courts)
2·30 Table tennis (Quarter finals only) - Sheila (Games room)

TUESDAY

AT SWIMMING POOL - MANDY

2·30 diving lesson
3·30 Water polo
4·30 Swimming (swimmers only)

AT THE FOOTBALL FIELD - BILL

2·30 Under 13 rounders
4·00 Over 13 rounders

AT THE GYMNASIUM - SANDRA

2·30 Volleyball
4·00 Basketball

OTHER ACTIVITIES

2·30 Horse Riding - Paul (meet at front door)
2·30 Under 13 archery - Chris (Front lawn)
3·30 Over 13 archery - Chris (Front lawn)
2·30 Rock climbing - Colin (meet in A2)
3·30 Table tennis - Sheila (games room).

WEDNESDAY

AT THE SWIMMING POOL - MANDY

2:30 Swimming class (for non-swimmers)
3:30 Over 13 Swimming
4:30 Under 13 Swimming

AT THE FOOTBALL FIELD - BILL

2:30 Under 13 football
4:00 Over 13 football

AT THE GYMNASIUM - SANDRA

2:30 Aerobics
3:30 Basketball training

OTHER ACTIVITIES

2:30 Tennis - Paul (Tennis courts)
2:30 Croquet - Neville (Meet in A2)
2:30 Golf - David (Meet at front door)

73

> **traditional sports** – football, volleyball, tennis
>
> **specialist sports** – horse riding, wind surfing, golf
>
> **leisure sports** – clock golf, French cricket, Frisbee
>
> **options** – photography, singing, painting, chess

In addition to the daily variety, the programme would vary from day to day. Obviously, some activities, like tennis, may be offered every day and others, like horse riding, only twice a week.

The sports programme should be as flexible as possible. It is impossible to predict which sports will be popular with a group of students so the organiser needs to be able to adapt the programme as it develops. You should prepare programmes for at least seven wet afternoons in a two week period. With luck you may not need to use all these plans but it is better to be prepared for the worst.

You will probably want to plan some competitive tournaments in different sports. These are useful as they build up enthusiasm and they can become 'events' which help to make the holiday course memorable. Some types of tournament take time to set up and to play so it is advisable to plan your tournament programme along with the sports programme before the students arrive.

8.2 Introducing the Sports programme

On the first day of lessons the students should be taken on a tour of the sports facilities in groups by their language teachers. This will be an opportunity for them to see what sports are available and to meet the sports staff. It is very valuable for the students to learn the names of the sports teachers and to become accustomed to their voices. When the students are asked to sign up for different sports the tour will have given them an idea of the different activities which are available.

8.3 Administering the Sports programme

The sports programme will probably have a large notice board in a prominent place in the school. This will be divided into sections for today's and tomorrow's programmes and for individual sports. Sporting magazines are an excellent source of illustrations for the posters promoting the different sports. Teachers might like to get the students to produce the posters. Students' involvement in administration encourages a sense of cohesion.

The noticeboard will be only one source of information. A short period during the language lessons each morning should be devoted to information about the sports programme. This can be done either by a member of the sports staff who will go around the classes or by the language teachers themselves. These should not be seen as an interruption of the language lessons or as a waste of time. English is being used for a clear communicative purpose and the presence of the language teacher will make it possible to clear up any comprehension problems or to develop follow up discussion. Teachers may also wish to make announcements during meals if this is possible.

8.4
Safety in sports

Safety must be the primary consideration of any teachers associated with sporting activities. A serious accident can ruin the reputation of a school and the career of the supervising teacher. Although the accident may have been caused by the student's foolishness, the school and teacher will be blamed. Part of the enjoyment of sports comes from pushing physical skills to the limit and so there is a constant danger that accidents will occur.

When accidents occur

1   Stop the activity

2   Isolate the student

3   Make a quick assessment of the injury

4   Apply first aid

5   Call assistance

6   Inform Course Director

7   Write a report

REMEMBER DR ABC!

D   Danger – water, fire, electricity, etc.
R   Resuscitation – kiss of life, etc.
A   Airways – clear and unrestricted?
B   Bleeding – stop it!
C   Concussion – any signs?

8.4.1
Planning for safety

The avoidance of accidents begins with the planning of the sports programme. Sports such as swimming and archery carry a greater degree of risk than tennis or basketball. The high-risk sports should only be offered on the programme if there will be a qualified member of staff present at all times when these activities are taking place. A bronze medallion life saver is of little use to a drowning child if the life saver is busy supervising a volleyball match.

Qualified sports staff can only be asked to supervise limited numbers of students doing a dangerous sport so the programme must be planned to offer alternatives when these activities are taking place.

8.4.2
Safety in
swimming

Since swimming is a very popular activity with students and is offered by most holiday courses, it deserves special attention. British law demands the presence of a qualified life saver whenever swimming is taking place. It is not enough to have a couple of 'good swimmers' – the law demands the qualification. Most trainee Physical Education Teachers will have taken and passed the bronze medallion qualification in their first year of training. This is the minimum acceptable qualification for all teachers of water sports and so schools that offer swimming in a private pool must employ someone with this qualification. This person must supervise all pool activities.

The swimming pool is a potentially dangerous place and so it is necessary to regulate the students' behaviour at the pool. These regulations are mostly common sense; no swimming directly after meals, no running on the side of the pool, no throwing of balls, floats or other objects, no 'bombing', no diving when the pool is being used for swimming and so on. There is no reason why these rules should not be taught as part of a language class before the students go to their swimming period. The language teachers will be more qualified to explain the rules in a way which is suitable to the linguistic ability of the students and to check that comprehension is achieved. Many pools are equipped with graphic posters which remind the users of these rules. If your pool does not have the posters, why not get the students to make them?

Public swimming pools are increasingly conscious of the threat of spreading diseases. Most have disinfectant foot baths in the corridors leading to and from the pool, some also insist on the use of some form of swimming cap. These are sensible precautions and are not difficult to apply.

Safety in the swimming pool can be improved by treating 'swimmers' and 'non-swimmers' separately, so the first job of the swimming teacher is to assess the ability of each student. When each group arrives at the pool show them the deep end and the shallow end. Ask the students who think they can swim a length to go to the deep end and demonstrate their ability. Watch out for those students who look hesitant. Don't let the students start from the shallow end! If they find they can only swim three-quarters of a length they will be out of their depth when they stop. The swimming teacher should take the names of the students who can swim a length of the pool. These 'swimmers' will be able to use the pool at different times from the non-swimmers. The school may have offered coaching for non-swimmers as one of its 'specialist sports' alternatives. Even if this has not been done it is advisable, for safety reasons, to treat the non-swimmers separately. You can use ropes to limit these students to the shallow part of the pool and you can give them the special help they need. There should be a supply of floats and inflatable arm bands. If the pool is not full, the non-swimmers are less likely to be frightened and the teacher can give his/her full attention to this group. Non-swimmers can easily take part in the swimming gala by competing in special events; walking across the shallow end of the pool, swimming across with a float in front of them, relay races and so on.

8.4.3
Organisation and discipline at the swimming pool

You will probably divide the pool time for each group into periods of an hour. When you allow for the time that the students will spend changing into their swimming costumes and back into their normal clothes this will probably allow about 40 minutes to each group. When students are changing and leaving their clothes in communal changing rooms it is not unusual for valuables to be lost and for this to lead to accusations of theft. It is a good idea for the swimming teacher to be equipped with a number of small plastic bags in order to take charge of watches, spectacles, money and other valuables. Young children often take ages to change and after a swimming lesson will reappear wearing their T shirts inside out and their shoes on the wrong feet. There is no reason why you should not organise 'getting dressed' lessons and competitions for these children.

As mentioned above, the basic rules of behaviour in the swimming pool can be taught by language teachers under the guidance of the swimming teacher. Communication in the swimming pool is often very difficult because of noise and dreadful acoustics. If you need to discipline any of the students, use a whistle to attract attention and to call the students to you by gesturing. Always get the students out of the pool and close to you before you try to speak to them. If you shout at the students, it will encourage them to shout at each other. Anyway, it is much easier to discipline the students in a calm voice.

8.4.4
What to do when accidents occur

Accidents will occur, so you should prepare yourself to deal with them. Stop the activity and get the other students to sit down. Seated students can cause less damage to themselves and others than those who are wandering around. Isolate the injured student from the rest of the group. Children and adults are often keen to dramatise their injuries in front of their colleagues. Look at the student and make a quick assessment of the severity of the injury. Bangs to the head and broken or twisted limbs should be treated with particular caution. Presumably you know how to give the kiss of life and to deal with arterial bleeding.

Remember that teenagers may be prone to fainting and epileptic fits. If a student does suffer a fit, it is generally better not to try to restrain him or her. Make plenty of space around the student and allow the fit to pass.

In any emergency send an adult or responsible student to get help. (You will, of course, know where that help can be obtained. A qualified sports teacher will have had training in first aid.) If the student is standing, make him or her sit down. Otherwise don't move the student in any way. Don't give the student anything to eat or drink. Loosen any tight clothing. Unless the injury is clearly superficial, contact a doctor. This will be better for your peace of mind and will protect you legally. As soon as the injury has been dealt with, make sure that you write a detailed report of the incident and give it to the director of the course. The parents of the injured student should be informed as soon as possible. Try to do this in a way which will minimise their distress. If the student has been sent through an agency, you should also advise them.

The other students in the school are very likely to tell their parents about the accident because, from their point of view, it is one of the exciting things that have happened. You should do your best to minimise the seriousness of the injury when speaking to other students because you can be sure that they will over-dramatise the incident when reporting it to their parents.

It is important to understand the point of view of the parents. The students are enjoying their first experience of being away from home. The parents are feeling guilty and worried about having put their children into the hands of unknown and possibly irresponsible foreigners. Their distress will be fuelled by the alarming stories they hear from their children and this will inevitably reflect badly on the school and the whole idea of holiday courses.

Whenever accidents and injuries occur your priorities should be

1]   to get qualified medical help for the injured student.

2]   to reduce distress and panic in the other students and the parents of the injured student.

3]   to protect yourself from legal action.

8.5
Team games

Many traditional team games are known and played throughout the world and are therefore popular on holiday course sports programmes. Team games have the added advantage of involving large numbers of players while requiring few adult supervisors. For example, one teacher would be able to supervise four teams of eleven students playing two football matches across the two halves of a standard football pitch. At the end of the games you can organise a match between the two winning teams and another between the losers. An alternative would be to have three teams, two playing and one watching. Each time a certain score is reached the losing team is replaced by the spectators. The new team have an obvious advantage because they are less tired. This encourages rapid play and maintains the interest of all the students.

When organising team games you should avoid national teams. The holiday course should be encouraging the mixing of nationalities so you don't want to promote xenophobia. After a short warm up period, choose the two, three or four best players (depending on the number of teams you need) and ask them to pick their teams from the group. At first, they may pick their friends, but very soon they will select on the basis of talent and you will find that you have multinational teams. Although some team games like football are more traditionally played by boys than girls, there is no reason why the teams should not be mixed. This policy should apply to all the sporting activities.

The students are likely to know team games like football, volleyball, basketball and possibly handball so you will not need to teach them. The holiday course should also be an opportunity to try something new. Depending on the equipment available you could introduce hockey (with a tennis ball), lacrosse (again with a tennis ball) or badminton (played by teams of five players on each side). Rounders is often very popular and is fairly easy to teach.

Students who are away from home do not expect things to be exactly the same as they are at home so you can introduce a twist to traditional games. For example, if you have mixed age groups playing football you might introduce a rule that in each team the attackers should be in the 11–14 age group while the defenders are 14–18. The defenders are not allowed to move beyond the half way line. Another way to add a twist is through some form of handicapping. This can be done through giving one team a scoring advantage, by having teams of unequal numbers, by limiting some players to certain parts of the playing area or by changing the size of the goals.

8.6 Individual games

Tennis is usually a popular option on holiday courses and many residential schools will have tennis courts available. Tennis requires minimal supervision and students can usually be allowed to play on their own if the courts are within the school grounds. If the students need to walk to courts at a distance from the school you will have to judge the safety of the journey. Think, not only of the roads which they will have to cross, but of possible harassment from local youths. Most of the students will not be accustomed to traffic driving on the left and may cross a road after looking the wrong way. A small group of young students dressed in light sports clothes wandering down a lonely street may well be in danger of sexual assault. They could also be approached in a perfectly innocent way, but because of their limited language ability they interpret this approach as being sexual. A school cannot afford to take this sort of risk.

Many schools have facilities for table tennis and this can be a popular activity both for afternoons and evenings. You could easily organise a table tennis ladder like the tennis ladder described in 8.10 below.

You might also be able to organise a five mile run one afternoon. This distance should be within the capability of most students over the age of fourteen. If you have younger students you can reduce the distance. Produce a nice looking certificate which can be awarded to all the students who complete the distance.

8.7 Sporting activities outside the school

In most areas you will be able to find sporting facilities outside the school. These may include riding schools, tennis or golf clubs, sailing clubs, ten-pin bowling centres, mini-golf parks, croquet lawns, ice skating rinks and often complete sports centres. The charges for using these facilities are not usually excessive and they can add considerable variety to your sports programme. You will probably need to plan these excursions in advance, particularly if you want to take large groups of students. In some of these centres you will find qualified instructors who can help the students. The use of these facilities outside the school will give the students a greater opportunity to meet ordinary people.

8.8 Non-competitive activities

Pop-ability is rather like a reduced form of aerobics. It combines the use of pop music with an energetic form of dancing. It is very popular with both boys and girls and can take place in any space with a fair sound system and a reasonable floor.

Some holiday courses also offer keep fit classes, gymnastics and self defence classes. These may demand some time in the gymnasium but it may be possible to do them outside in good weather.

As mentioned in the chapter on social activities some of the staff might be interested in taking small groups of students on a short walk to investigate the local wildlife or geology, to look at architecture, to do photography or sketching. In some areas there can be organised visits to local farms. When planning the programme you should work with the social director – you have to think of the students who don't like any sports!

8.9
Wet weather

As I mentioned before you should plan a programme of wet weather activities. You will have to look carefully at the facilities available both inside and outside which can be done on wet days. You might consider organising a swimming gala or a short volleyball tournament in the gymnasium. Many students will enjoy watching as much as playing. Remember to consider the non-sporting alternatives such as an afternoon disco, a visit to the local cinema and so on.

8.10
Tournaments and Competitions

The main problem with most tournaments is that the best student always wins. The less gifted students are reluctant to participate because they feel they have no hope of winning. Since in the holiday course you want the maximum number to be involved, it is a good idea to introduce a handicapping system so that the weaker students can win. Obviously in order to do this you need to have an idea of each student's ability. If you are considering a tennis tournament in the second week of a two week course, you could organise a tennis ladder during the first week. The ladder starts as a list of students probably placed in order of age. The idea of the tennis ladder is that any player may challenge another player up to five steps above in the ladder. If the lower placed player wins then he/she exchanges positions with the higher placed player. The ladder has the advantage that no player gets knocked out and stops participating. The result of the tennis ladder after the first week will be a guidance for the handicapping system in the tournament. It is a good challenge for a competent player to start each game at love-fifteen when playing against a weaker opponent.

8.10.1
The Finals

The final of a tournament can make a popular spectator event towards the end of a course. The prizes could be awarded at the disco later in the evening. It is a good idea to make the prize-giving a formal event because it makes the tournament more memorable and makes all the students feel more involved. Prizes should be awarded to all the students who participate. The prizes can vary from certificates to badges, medals or cups. These can be bought quite cheaply from sports shops. You may also consider taking photographs of the students receiving their prizes.

8.11
Language involvement in sports

Students on holiday courses will spend many hours of each day using English. We should remember that this is very tiring and so we should not try to impose language work on the sporting activities. Part of the reason for having the periods devoted to sport is to give the students a rest from the foreign language.

Some use of English will arise naturally from the sporting activities because the sports staff will need to explain, control, encourage and discipline. It would be a good idea for the sports teachers to sit in on one or two lessons so that they can learn the best way to speak to foreign students. Language teachers will understand the communicative advantages which sports teachers have because most things can be shown or demonstrated.

There are plenty of opportunities to integrate the sports and language programmes. We have already mentioned that the language class can be used for explaining a new game and for teaching the code of conduct in the swimming pool. At some point during the language lessons each day the students may be asked to read and complete forms expressing their preferences for sports alternatives that afternoon. This can be a stimulus for useful discussion and introducing the language of likes, dislikes and preferences.

8.11.1
Language
teachers'
involvement in
sports

In schools where there are specialist sports staff the language teachers' involvement should be limited to sports in which they are qualified or experienced. Language teachers who have no sports qualifications should never be asked to supervise dangerous sports. However if they are interested and willing to help, their participation should be welcomed.

**8.12
Conclusion**

Sporting activities are traditionally an important part of a successful holiday language course. They provide many opportunities for students to observe and use language in action and so they are an important contribution to the students' language development. Many people would argue that the students gain more language outside the classroom than they do during the lessons and there are good reasons for thinking that this might be the case.

WELFARE

The major area of complaint about holiday language courses is welfare. This is not strange because the students are not in a position to judge whether they have been well taught or whether the leisure programme has been imaginative, however they all feel qualified to judge if the accommodation has been satisfactory and the food ample and edible.

Sometimes national group leaders have been known to exacerbate the students' dissatisfaction with food or accommodation and since they have a major welfare role, I have included the chapter on group leaders in this section.

9

Accommodation

**9.0
Types of
accommodation**

Students who are attending holiday courses are usually housed in residential accommodation or with host families. Less frequently, the students may stay in hostels, hotels or self-catering apartments. A few holiday course students may be living with local friends or with their parents.

**9.1
Residential
accommodation**

Holiday course organisations often rent the premises of private residential schools during the summer. These schools usually provide dormitory accommodation although some schools have study bedrooms for individuals or pairs of students. The 'spartan' tradition, so often associated with private education in Britain, is unknown to most foreign students and they may well be shocked by the primitive nature of dormitories, bathrooms and lavatories. Since there is nothing that can be done to improve these facilities the staff should try to give the students the idea that these conditions are part of the adventure of being in Britain. Students who have never experienced the communal adventure of a scout camp may initially find it difficult to settle down in these conditions. If the staff spend their time talking about how dreadful the place is, the students are unlikely to be happy. If, however, they talk about what fun it is for the students to be together, the students will quickly enter into the spirit of the school.

9.1.1 Sleeping accommodation	Whether the school has dormitories or smaller rooms, male and female students should be separated in some way. This is often done by females occupying one floor or wing while males are housed in another. As far as possible the language groups should be mixed in the rooms so that the students are encouraged to use English. If there are very young children in the school, it is better not to mix them with the older students. The younger ones will probably go to sleep earlier and the older students are likely to keep them awake. It is very important that the residential areas should be kept as tidy as possible. It is very difficult for the cleaners to do a reasonable job if the students do not keep their rooms tidy. There is also a greater chance that possessions will get lost or stolen in an untidy room. The school students who normally live in those rooms throughout the year are expected to keep them tidy so there is no reason why the same rules should not apply to the foreign students. The students should make their beds every morning (you may have to teach them how to do this), put their suitcases, etc. on the bed (to clear the floor for cleaning) and put away their clothes. If you think it is necessary, you can introduce a competition for the tidiest room. It is very difficult for students to keep their rooms tidy if there is not adequate space to store their clothes and personal possessions. It is also important that there should be places where clothes can be hung up to dry otherwise you will find swimming costumes and underwear hanging on radiators and out of windows. You should make strict rules about the storage and consumption of food in dormitories. There is no point in the kitchen staff following the food hygiene regulations if the students go back to their bedrooms and eat, dropping crumbs, if nothing more. There is also the danger of attracting mice.
9.1.2 Bathrooms and lavatories	There should be an adequate number of bathrooms and lavatories for the students but they may be lacking the privacy which many students might expect. If this is the case, you may have to establish a rota of different times when the students can use the bathrooms. If the school is normally a single sex boys' school, the accommodation officer may have to check that there are sufficient lavatories for the girls. It may also be necessary to provide a supply of sanitary towels and provide for their hygienic disposal. Bathrooms and lavatories should be kept clean and checked daily.
9.1.3 Staff accommodation	In residential schools it is normal for the staff to be housed in private rooms which are close to the students' accommodation. These staff members often have to do some supervision. If you are asked to take on this responsibility, not much actual supervision should be required provided that you explain the procedures clearly when the students arrive.

Very young students may be a little tearful in the first evenings and should be comforted. In fact this homesickness is often caused by speaking to the parents on the telephone.

It may be necessary to check the tidiness of the bedrooms from time to time but if you establish a routine the students should be able to stick to it. You should be careful on the last night of the course as the boys are likely to invade the girls' dormitories.

Symptoms of Homesickness

There may be many reasons for the following behaviour patterns but they could be an indication of homesickness.

Doesn't join in activities.

Doesn't eat.

Excessive consumption of sweet foods or drinks.

Complains of cold.

Doesn't sleep or sleeps excessively.

Cries.

Wets bed.

Constant complaints of minor sickness.

Poor attendance at lessons or other activities.

Day dreaming in lessons or at meal times.

Frequent phone calls to or from parents.

Sitting alone clasping knees and rocking.

Unwilling to contact parents.

Stubborn.

Aggressive towards staff, family or other students.

9.1.4
Laundry

Students who are involved in many activities will get through a large amount of clothing. Laundry should be collected twice weekly and returned the next day. An alternative would be for the students to have access to washing and drying machines on the premises. When laundry is being done outside the school it is a good idea to have labelled black plastic bags to collect the dirty washing from each dormitory. The students' clothes are unlikely to have name tags.

9.1.5
Wake up time
and bed time

You should not need to worry about waking most students. However, some may need a little encouragement if they are not to miss breakfast. These students can be quickly identified and you can give another student the responsibility to wake them.

Students will probably spend a lot of time talking after lights out during the first few nights of the course. This may disturb students who want to sleep. There is no way to prevent students from talking, they naturally want to get to know each other, but they can be asked to have some consideration for their companions.

Your decision on bed times will have to be based on the ages of the students. Remember that in continental Europe children often go to bed later than British children of the same age. Don't let the students stay up too late, because tired children are more likely to have accidents. You will also need to sleep!

9.1.6
Fire regulations

If you are using the premises of a private school, they should have been inspected and passed for fire safety. Make sure that fire doors are kept shut and that the fire extinguishers are in position. Instructions for the evacuation of the building in case of fire must be displayed in every classroom, dormitory, lounge and dining room and all areas used by the students. These procedures should be explained to the students and, because of linguistic problems, you should show the students how they should leave. A fire practice can be an enjoyable adventure for the students. Before the first fire practice tell the students that it is going to occur. Tell them to expect another fire practice during their stay. Then you can hold a second fire practice at your own convenience.

9.1.7
Communal areas

There should be a variety of lounges and other common rooms which the students can use. One of these should contain a television and perhaps a video. Providing copies of the *Radio Times* and *TV Times* will give extra reading practice for the students. Newspapers which have been used in lessons can also be put in the television room. Another room should have some sort of cassette player. There is no need to provide many cassettes, the students will bring their own.

As you walk around the school make sure that corridors and stairways are clean and adequately lit. The best way to avoid litter is to provide plenty of litter bins.

9.2
Host families

A popular alternative to residential accommodation is provided by host families. These families are paid a weekly fee by the school in exchange for taking one or more students as guests in their homes. If a family takes more than one student, the accommodation officer will try to make sure that the students speak different languages. Students who share a mother tongue should only be placed in the same family by special request. The arrangements may vary from bed and breakfast to full board. There may also be combinations which provide half-board on weekdays and full-board at weekends.

When host family accommodation works well, it can be the most enjoyable and linguistically beneficial arrangement for the students. They share the home life of the host family, being with them for meals and joining in all the family's activities. This provides an exceptional opportunity for the students to learn about day-to-day life in Britain and to make friends with ordinary British people.

In a residential school there is always a danger that the students will only meet a few British teachers and other foreign students. They will have no close contact with the general population of Britain. Host family accommodation overcomes this problem. In general, the host families take their job seriously and are very conscious of their successes and failures.

A successful stay with a host family requires contributions from both the family and the students. The family must allow the students to participate in family life and should be prepared to make some adjustments to the needs of the students. Equally, the students should not treat the host family as a hotel. They must be willing to try to communicate in English, to eat British food and adapt to the British way of life. As one host family member said, 'I feel I have failed if I am forced to speak Italian to Italian students and to provide them with Italian food. I am willing to adapt to their ways, but this means that they are not getting any benefit from being with a British family. They might as well have stayed at home.'

9.2.1 How are the host families chosen?

In most schools which use host family accommodation, there is an accommodation officer who is responsible for finding the families, inspecting them and then supervising the placement and welfare of the students. Families are found through advertisements in shops or local newspapers or leaflets pushed through the door. The family then applies and fills in a questionnaire giving details of the house, the family members, pets, working habits and so on. The family may also express preferences for the type of students they would like to host. The accommodation officer will then go to visit the family, look at the rooms available and talk about the responsibilities of the host family. The selected families are usually given a leaflet which gives them guidance in their treatment of the students. The ARELS/FELCO organisation produces an excellent booklet which is available to members. Accommodation officers usually have a large card index system which gives details of all the families they use regularly because most families continue to host students year after year.

In some areas it is now becoming increasingly difficult to find suitable host families for the number of students who wish to come to Britain. For this reason alone good host families should be treasured and treated as well as possible. Some schools hold a reception for the host families during the course and invite them to attend entertainments such as the 'International Evening'. If there are teenagers in the families they can also be invited to discos and so on. It is very important for the school to demonstrate that they recognise the important role the host families play in the success of the holiday courses.

Family Reference Card

NAME **Rogers**

      Grade **A**

ADDRESS **17, Connaught Road, Cosham PO3 3TY**

TEL **0705-134429**

BUS ROUTE **261A**

RESIDENT FAMILY MEMBERS

MRS EILEEN ROGERS, Geography Teacher

MR FRANK ROGERS, Civil Servant

PAUL ROGERS, 12

DANIEL ROGERS, 10

SMOKING **No**   PETS **None**

ROOMS AVAILABLE **2 singles**

Special Diets **No**   Smokers **No**

REMARKS

Prefers young male students during school holidays

DATE OF INFORMATION **12/6/89**
DATE OF LAST VISIT **12/6/89**

My father works in a factory, which makes fridges. He's the technical director.
My mother is a computer operator. She works for SIP, SIP is the italian telephone company.
My brother Giorgio is at university. He is learning law.
My brother Sergio is at Liceo.

9.2.2
Arriving at the host family

Students who go to host families should be prepared to communicate. The first stage is breaking the ice. When they first arrive they will probably be offered a cup of tea or coffee and they will be asked 'Did you have a good journey?' The host family is trying to be friendly and expressing this friendliness in a typically British way. The student who refuses the drink and answers the enquiry with monosyllables will be rejecting the hand of friendship which has been offered. Even worse is the student who accepts the tea or coffee and then turns his nose up in disgust at the taste. If the student does not like tea or coffee, it is much better to say 'Could I have a glass of water?' It is a good idea for the student to create an arrival 'pack' – a map showing where they live, photographs of their town and different members of their family, perhaps a gift of a local product for the host family. This pack will provide the visual aids for the first ice-breaking conversation. Preferably, the student should practise this conversation with a teacher before they go to Britain. Do they know the vocabulary to describe their mother's or father's profession? Do they know how to describe where they live? Do they know how to talk about their journey to Britain?

The next step is the tour of the house. The student must know how to make appreciative comments when they are being shown round. 'What a lovely room!' and 'That's beautiful wallpaper!' may seem like clichés, but they are excellent formulae for establishing a friendly relationship. They must also remember to say 'please' and 'thank-you' as often as possible.

9.2.3
Food in host families

The student that really annoys the host family is the one who refuses to try anything which he or she has never seen before. The families are usually accustomed to having foreign guests and are very willing to adapt to special needs but the students must be able to explain what these are. The student should have a good bilingual dictionary which will give the names of popular food stuffs. The holiday course teachers should also help in this respect by teaching students the language they need to talk about food. Host families know that eggs and cheese are usually safe and that bread and fruit should always be provided. Students who are prepared to try will always find new things that they like and once again they should express their appreciation.

It is polite to inform the host families if they are going to be late for meals.

9.2.4 Travelling to and from the host family

Accommodation officers usually try to select homes which are within easy reach of the school. In the busiest months of the summer they often have to use homes which are further from the school but there should be an adequate public transport service. This may be satisfactory during the day but schools should be careful when students are returning home after evening activities. Very often the families are willing to come and collect the students in the same way as they would with their own children.

9.2.5 Coming home late	Some schools tell the students when they should be back with their host families if they have been out in the evening. Many accommodation officers tell the families to treat the students as they would their own children of that age. Obviously the host families will know more than the students about local dangers like drug pushers and hooligans.

Some schools ask the host families to provide the students with a house key but most leave it to the discretion of the family.

Some schools provide the host families with a copy of the social programme each week so that they know in advance when to expect the students to come home.

9.2.6 Dealing with problems	If a host family has a problem with a student they will usually contact the accommodation officer who will deal with it. If a student is unhappy with the host family a teacher or group leader is likely to be the first to hear of it. These problems should always be referred to the accommodation officer. He (or more often, she) has the expertise in dealing with these difficulties. They are frequently trivial and only caused by misunderstanding. If it is justified the accommodation officer will move the student to another family.

9.2.7 Language and host families	It is very difficult for the students to join in with family life if they feel they have nothing to say. Language teachers can help the student's integration with the family. The students can be asked to find out information about their host families.

'What kind of car have they got?'
'What time do they go to work?'
'Where do they work?', etc.

Obviously the teacher should avoid invading the privacy of the families. The students should not appear to be spying on their host families. However, if you keep to fairly neutral topics you can stimulate some useful language interchange.

Students can also find out their host family's opinions on different topics.

'What is their favourite television programme/film/actor/foreign country/type of music?'

Once again you should avoid sensitive topics.

10

Food

10.0
Introduction

This chapter is addressed chiefly to administrators and course directors but since the discussion of food often dominates holiday courses, it will be of interest to all members of the teaching and welfare staff. Section 10.4 is addressed particularly to language teachers.

10.1
Will the students complain about British food?

Food is the most frequent cause for complaint on holiday courses. There is no good reason for this – and that makes the problem even worse. British food has improved in the past ten years with a greater variety of foodstuffs being available and more interest being shown in the preparation of interesting dishes. Part of the value of going abroad is to experience the food and habits of the foreign country but all people display a basic conservatism which is most frequently manifested through their eating habits. The British make fun of their compatriots who demand fish and chips in Minorca. Foreign students in language schools are no different. They like (and trust) what they get at home and they are often unwilling to experiment. This behaviour is not limited to children, adults can be the most vocal protesters.

There are three lines of argument which school staff can adopt when speaking to students:
(a) You will not die from eating British food for three weeks.
(b) You should suggest politely how the food could be made more appetising. (e.g. ask for bread with your meals or ask your host family if you can dress your salad.)
(c) Always ask to try a small portion before you are served with a standard portion. You will probably find many things which you like.

10.2
Food on residential courses

When a holiday course operation moves into a school or college they are usually expected to use the same catering staff who work there for the rest of the year. The local staff will obviously have their standard procedures and styles of work and the holiday course will be expected to fit in with these as far as possible. The standard menus for the students who usually eat their food may not be acceptable to foreign students but any negotiations with the caterers will have to be handled delicately. They will often suggest producing spaghetti or other British attempts at foreign foods – avoid this if at all possible!

**10.2.1
Breakfast**

Breakfast may well be the apex of British cooking but do not be surprised if some students cannot face the idea of greasy, cooked food at that time in the morning. Make sure that there is plenty of toast and marmalade available and gradually try to persuade the students towards the delights of bacon and sausages.

**10.2.2
Packed lunches
on excursions**

The notes on packed lunches provided by host families below should also apply to those provided by the kitchen of a residential school. The excursion staff should remember that many young students suffer from travel sickness during long coach journeys and this can be aggravated by eating stodgy sandwiches and drinking fizzy drinks. You will not be able to prevent this but a supply of sickness bags and fresh water can prevent the problem from becoming a crisis.

**10.2.3
Main meals**

In main meals, concentrate on foods which require the minimum preparation. Food which is in its raw state is less likely to be visually unacceptable to the students. Cold meats and salads are always popular and you can offer a considerable variety. Most overseas students prefer their salad dressed with oil and vinegar so make these available to them. Students will usually eat eggs and they are a good source of protein. Try to make sure that fresh fruit is always available. Tell the students that the fruit has been washed but do not be surprised if they want to wash it again. Jelly and custard, those two standbys of British children's food, will be greeted with amazement and disgust by many foreign students.

**10.2.4
Snacks**

The kitchen staff may be accustomed to serving the evening meal between six and seven in the evening. They will often be unwilling to change their routines to prepare a later meal. In this case try to make sure that some light snacks (biscuits and a cold drink) are available to the students later in the evening. Mediterranean students would be accustomed to eating at about nine in the evening and would certainly get hungry at about this time.

**10.2.5
Staff meals**

If possible staff should eat with the students so that they can encourage experimentation and watch for the students who are intent on starving themselves to death. You should be very careful about pressurising students to eat food they do not like. It is so easy to think that you are being encouraging while the student feels constrained. Teachers can also stimulate some useful language exchanges at mealtimes.

**10.2.6
Organisation of
meal times**

Many residential courses have moved over to a self-service canteen system. This generally works well but can lead to long queues of noisy and unruly students waiting to be served. Staggering the meal times can help considerably if this is a problem. Some schools put notice boards beside the queue so that the students have something to look at while they are waiting.

Self service does lead to more food being wasted. Students will tend to take more food than they can eat or, having taken it, discover that they do not like it. It may also discourage some students from experimenting with unfamiliar food as there may not be the possibility to take a small portion and then go back for more.

Bread should be available at all meals. If possible this should not be the standard British white, sliced loaf. It is not too difficult to obtain more interesting and appetising types of bread.

If the self-service organisation means that students should clear their own trays, be sure to show the students how this should be done.

Menu

10.2.7 Special diets	For religious, medical or cultural reasons some students follow special diets. In order to allow them to do this, it is better to explain what a prepared food contains. A Muslim student, in a self-service canteen, asked at the cash desk if the meat was pork. 'No, it isn't,' he was assured, 'it's ham.' The poor man took the plate and was later very upset at having eaten forbidden meat.

You usually get notice if any students are on special diets but, to be on the safe side, a vegetarian alternative should be available at all meals.

10.3 **Food in host** **families**	Host families, who accept foreign students, will do their best to content the needs of their guests. If the students have chosen to be accommodated with a host family then they should try to accept what that family offers. The preferences of the family members will usually govern the family menu, but most families will be willing to adapt to the special needs of their guests.

Students should not imagine that they are staying in a hotel with an à la carte menu. They cannot order the food which they would like. Very often unhappiness with food may be the result of language problems.

10.3.1 **Packed lunches**	Some non-residential schools ask the host families to give the students a packed lunch. These may be quite interesting to begin with but after a time the students find them repetitive. Encourage the host families to experiment with different types of bread and there are a wide variety of fillings which can be used for sandwiches. Crisps are usually popular. Some students also like yoghurt. Fresh fruit is usually very acceptable.

10.4 **Food and** **language**	Language teachers should devote some lessons to talking about food. It provides a rich area of useful vocabulary – students need to be able to name the foods they like and those they don't. More importantly (and particularly for students with host families) they need to be able to express their likes and dislikes *politely*. They need to be able to ask permission and make suggestions without causing offence. They should know how to express enthusiasm for the food they are given. We all know that a good way to show enthusiasm is to ask for the recipe. This can be done rudely:

    'What's in this?'

or politely:

    'How do you make this?'

At all times we should try to prevent food becoming a source of friction.

10.4.1 Politeness	Politeness is a means by which we oil the wheels of interaction. The basic, 'neutral' language which elementary students often learn can sound very abrupt when used in a social setting. Students can use the opportunity of the holiday course to develop a little more gentility in their speech.

The dinner table provides a useful stimulus for language which can be transferred to other settings. The function of asking for something can be developed:

'More carrots!'

'Give me more carrots.'

'I want some more carrots.'

'I want some more carrots, please.'

'I'd like some more carrots, please'

'Could I have some more carrots, please?'

These linguistic convolutions will not surprise the students. In their own languages, there are similar linguistic formulae for expressing politeness.

Teaching the students to be polite in English will benefit them both linguistically and socially. Host families are just as worried about the students as the students are about the host families. The student who does not seem to like the food being offered makes the host family feel it is not fulfilling its role. If this is combined with failure to communicate, the resulting tension may well spill over into other areas of the relationship.

10.5
Junk food

Many schools operate a shop where students can buy sweets, soft drinks and other forms of junk food. Staff should look out for students who are refusing main meals and spending fortunes on crisps and sweets. An excessive intake of junk food over a short period is not going to cause much damage but this behaviour could be indicative of some other underlying problem. It would be worth investigating with tact.

10.6
Food in bedrooms

Students should be discouraged from hoarding food in their bedrooms, particularly if the food is unwrapped. This can encourage mice and other vermin and has led to groups cancelling their contracts with the school.

10.7
Food and sports

Many students are rightly conscious of the dangers of swimming after a heavy meal. Less well known are the dangers of dehydration which may follow long periods of strenuous activity in hot weather. Sports organisers should follow the rule that students should never be forced to do something against their will but they should sometimes be prevented from doing things which are against their interests.

11

Group leaders

**11.0
The value of
group leaders**

Group leaders can ruin a holiday course. They can also contribute greatly to its success. This chapter is intended to assist both schools and group leaders to collaborate in making the holiday course as enjoyable and useful for the students as possible. Unfortunately, there is frequently a lack of understanding between schools and group leaders which can lead to unnecessary conflict. The purpose of this chapter is both to help group leaders and to give schools a better understanding of the group leader's role.

11.0.1
Who are the
group leaders?

A group leader usually accompanies a number of students who come from the same country and share the same language. The group may come from the same town, from the same study tours agency, or even from the same school. The group leader may be the regular English language teacher of the group. The group leader may be a professional English language teacher or perhaps a University student who has taken on this responsibility as a summer vacation job.

**11.1
The role of the
group leader**

The job of the group leader is to act as a link between the students' home culture and that of the country they are visiting. Their job is not simply to translate when translation is necessary but to guide and comfort the students in meeting the new culture. They are employed, partly, to reassure parents who are anxious about sending their children alone to a foreign country. Parents can imagine amazing misfortunes which might occur and they worry that there may be no native speaker of their own language who can assist the child and inform them of the problem.

11.1.1
Learning about
the students

If you are going to guide and assist a group of students you will need to collect a lot of information about them. You will need to know their names, ages, telephone numbers and addresses. You will need to know where their parents can be contacted during the time the group will be away. Do not assume that you can get this information from the student in an emergency, – the student may be unconscious! It is also useful to know about any special problems which each student has. Do they walk in their sleep? Do they have to follow a special diet or take any medication? Are they frightened of dogs? Do you know the passport or identity card number of each student? Have you got a photograph of each student? Try to build up a file which contains all this information. If you can build up this file it will help you to anticipate and avoid many problems which may occur.

Group Leader's Record Card

Name *Stefania ROSSI*

DoB *13.6.77*

Passport/ID *67705513*   Height *1 m 38*

Address *Via F Casati 19, 20124 Milano 02-1413524*

Host Family *Rogers, 17 Connaught Road, Cosham*

Tel *0705-134429*

Special Notes *Allergic to aspirin*

11.1.2
The students'
expectations

It is sometimes difficult for an adult to understand the innocence of a child. All the students will have some expectations about the country they are going to visit. Maybe they have been brought up on Sherlock Holmes and they imagine that London is always in dense fog. Perhaps they imagine that all American or British people look like their favourite pop stars or the characters in their English language text books. It is difficult to understand these expectations but it would be a mistake to deny that they exist.

The contrast between these expectations and the reality of life in an English-speaking country will be the major source of culture shock and dissatisfaction. If it is possible, try to meet the students as a group, before the date of departure. This will give you an opportunity to get to know the students and to prepare them for their experience. At this meeting try to learn the name of each student and make a note of the potential trouble makers – the students who fight, the students who wander away from the group, the friendless students. You will also be able to spot the natural leaders in the group who, if they are responsible, can help you enormously.

This meeting may be the last time you see the students before you meet at the airport so you might consider giving them a checklist of things to pack. Remind the students to bring suitable clothing for the climate. Some students may wish to take a camera to record their holiday. Some will inevitably want to bring cassette players and their favourite music. The students will have to pack to certain weight restrictions so advise them not to overload themselves with bags and suitcases. This is particularly important because most students return from their holidays with more luggage than they took. You might even suggest that they pack an empty bag to allow for this need.

Checklist of things to Pack
The group leader might prepare a list like this in the students' mother tongue.

Clothes
Don't forget – warm sweater, raincoat or anorak, shoes for walking and sports, a good purse for money and valuables.

Sports
Don't forget your tennis racket if you want to play tennis, swimming costume, towel for swimming.

General
Dont forget you camera and some film, pens and pencils, addresses of your friends, your arrival pack, a present for your host family, your watch.

AND PLEASE DON'T FORGET YOUR PASSPORT/ID CARD AND YOUR MONEY!

Tell the students about the customs restrictions they will face. In particular, remind them that there is no duty free allowance for tobacco or alcohol for travellers under eighteen even if the goods are not for their consumption.

If the students are going to be staying with host families you can talk about the arrival pack of maps, photographs and gifts which is described in Chapter 9. An arrival pack will provide a useful stimulus in becoming friendly with the host family.

11.1.3
At the airport

The meeting at the airport will be a testing time for the group leader. Many of the students will come to the airport with their parents and the parents will take this opportunity to judge the person who will be looking after their children. Try to dress smartly and look professional. Try to look as if you are in charge of the situation, even if there is chaos around you. At this point you will need to reassure the parents who will come and ask you to take special care of their offspring.

When all the students have arrived check their names from your list. Don't just count them because you may be counting a brother or sister who is not a member of your group. The students will obviously be very excited – both eager and hesitant to leave their parents. In this situation it is useful to give the students something to do. You may be able to issue the students with special luggage labels to identify their cases and bags. Alternatively, give the students rolls of coloured adhesive tape to wrap around their luggage so that it will be easy to identify when they reach the baggage reclaim area at their destination.

As soon as you have collected your group together, take them through passport control to the departure lounge. Here, there is plenty to look at and do so you are less likely to lose any students. Before they spend all their money in the duty-free shop remind them of the customs restrictions – in particular on alcohol and tobacco products for passengers under 18 years of age. The last thing you want on arrival is trouble with customs. If any of the students have forgotten to buy gifts for their host families, they will probably be able to find some nice hand soap in the duty free shop.

About a quarter of an hour before the departure time collect your students together and take them to the departure gate. Remember that it is easier to count the students if they are sitting down. If they are standing and wandering around it is very easy to count one student twice. Try to make sure that all the students have used the lavatory before the flight because you don't want them moving around in the aircraft. The students will have been given their seat numbers for the plane and you should insist that they occupy those seats. Before going to the plane, you should explain to the students that they will have to put their hand baggage in the overhead baggage compartments or underneath the seat in front of them.

11.1.4
On the plane

When the students arrive at the plane try to get them seated as quickly as possible. Chewing gum is often useful for overcoming the air pressure on take off and landing. Some students may have decided to take travel sickness pills before the flight. On long flights it is most important to drink plenty of non-alcoholic liquids. Many of the students may be flying for the first time and feel nervous. During the flight, try to move around and reassure those students. You may have to discipline students who are over-excited. The cabin staff in the aircraft have a hard enough job without trying to control your group of students.

<table>
<tr><td>

11.1.5
Arriving

</td><td>

Some students may have to complete immigration control cards before landing. You may have to help the students to do this. When you land the students will have to go through immigration control. For students going to Britain from European Community countries this should be no problem. Those from some other countries may need a letter from the school in Britain which proves that they are going to attend a language course. They may also have to show their return air ticket. Try to place yourself in front of your group in the immigration queue so that you can explain the situation to the immigration officer and help individual students.

After immigration, lead the students to the baggage arrival area. If the students have labelled their bags and cases properly there should be no problems here, but check that the students have collected *all their luggage*. You will have checked that all of the students can go through the green customs channel so you can lead all of them through in a single group. Tell the students not to carry baggage belonging to other students.

When you come out of customs you will probably have to look for the representative of the school who will show your group to the coach which will take them to the school. Unless there is plenty of time to spare try to avoid the long queues to change money. This can be done in a local bank near the school.

When you have contacted the representative of the school, you will be able to find out if there is to be any delay in starting your coach journey to the school. Sometimes, during the busiest travel periods you may find that you have to wait for another group who will be using the same coach. If this is the case you can help the students to change money. Show them where the toilets are situated because they will probably need to use them. In the arrival lounge there are usually a wide range of shops and many of the students will be eager to explore and buy. After being confined in the aircraft for some time the students may tend to wander off. Try to prevent them from doing this because when the delayed group arrives you will want to be able to leave immediately.

</td></tr>
<tr><td>

11.1.6
First contacts
with the school

</td><td>

The remarks on coach journeys in Chapter 3 on excursions apply equally to your journey to the school. The students are likely to be tired and most will be content to look out of the windows. Remember that some students, who travelled by plane with no ill effects, may be travel sick on the coach.

As soon as you arrive at the school introduce yourself to the teachers and organisers. Don't take up too much of their time because they will be very busy. Your students will probably be offered a cup of tea or another drink when they arrive. You will notice at this time that your group will tend to stick together. This is quite natural at this stage so don't try to force them to mix with other students immediately.

If your students are going to be staying with host families, they will probably meet them for the first time at the school. The students standing

</td></tr>
</table>

in groups will look at the host families and you will overhear comments like 'Aren't they old?' and 'I hope I don't get that one.' These remarks are just an indication of the students' lack of confidence and so you shouldn't take them too seriously. Before the students leave, try to meet each family and introduce yourself. Check that you have the correct address and telephone number of each family. The students will feel happier if they know that there is some link between you and the host family.

If the students are going to be in residential accommodation, try to get them settled down as quickly as possible.

11.1.7 Starting the course

During the first few days of the course most of the problems which occur and need your assistance will be trivial. They will range from students who feel they have been placed in the wrong class, to those who are unhappy with the food or accommodation. These problems are usually just indications that the students are finding it difficult to adjust to the new situation. Look out for the symptoms of anxiety or homesickness listed in Chapter 6. You should try to encourage the sense of adventure and exploration which should be maintained throughout the holiday course. Try to minimise the discomforts and point out the positive aspects.

You should get to know the teachers and other members of the school staff and the leaders of other groups. In your relations with these people, express an interest in their work, show a willingness to cooperate but be careful not to imply that you want to interfere. Remember that they are also professionals in their work and you should take the opportunity to learn from them. You may have special interests or skills which would be useful to the school as a whole and you can mention these to the relevant members of staff.

11.2 Your responsibilities during the course

The most successful and useful group leaders are those who integrate with the life of the school as a whole. You will obviously have a special sense of responsibility towards your own group but if you appear to be joining in with the school activities, your group will also be more inclined to mix with the other students.

Holiday course operations have different policies on the responsibilities of group leaders. With some you may be required to do everything: teaching, sports, excursions and welfare. Some ask group leaders to take charge of their students when they are not having lessons or meals. Many organisations will only ask you to assist with excursions and with the welfare of the group.

If the first few days of the course you should try to find out what the school expects you to do. If you think these responsibilities are excessive then you should say so and tell the school what you are prepared to do. It is only fair that each side should know what they can be asked to do. Schools sometimes complain that certain group leaders are lazy but this is often the result of not clarifying the division of responsibilities at an early stage.

Your students will come to you with complaints but these should always be referred to the relevant member of the school staff. If the student is likely to have language difficulties in explaining the problem, you may choose to accompany the student. In these situations do not give the impression that you are complaining on behalf of the student – you are merely helping the student to explain the problem. You may be asked to act as a link with the parents of a student. In this case you should reassure the parents that the student is fit and healthy and, once again, try to minimise the problem.

The least successful group leaders are those who maximise the severity of every problem and encourage a sense of dissatisfaction in the group. These group leaders are excessively protective and argue with teachers, other members of the school staff and the leaders of other groups. They ruin the holiday course for their own group and often have a negative influence on the course as a whole.

11.3
The cultural link

During the holiday course you will be acting as a cultural link between the group's home culture and the new culture they are meeting. In this role, you can help the students to understand and appreciate life in the English-speaking country by putting their experiences into a context which they will understand. On excursions you can guide the students in making links between the things they see and learn about, and their experience at home. You should stress similarities rather than differences and in this way contribute to the benefit and enjoyment of the holiday course.

11.4
Serious problems

Remember that the best method of dealing with problems is to anticipate and avoid them. Any serious problems which occur will probably concern health or the police. Chapter 5 on sporting activities deals extensively with safety in sport and you should insist that the students obey the rules and avoid dangerous activities. Accidents often occur when students are crossing roads because they are not accustomed to traffic driving on the left. Apart from accidents other health problems may arise from allergies and infections. In all cases make sure that the student gets qualified medical help and if the problem is serious you should always contact the parents and consider sending the child home.

The other main area in which serious problems can occur concerns the police. Young people who are away from their parents feel that they are liberated from home restrictions. When they are in a group, they are more likely to attempt to steal from a shop or try an illicit drug as a way of showing off to the rest of the group. They may feel, for example, that a law which says that they must be eighteen years old to buy alcohol is ridiculous. Maybe the law is ridiculous, but it is the law and the students must respect it.

In general, you should have no problems in dealing with the police. They may speak sharply and try to frighten the student but as long as you show that you recognise the seriousness of the situation, you should have no problems. If you feel that the student has been falsely accused then you should explain this to the school and the police without getting angry or upset. Try to avoid being involved or trying to defend the student. Limit your involvement to translating if this is necessary.

If a student gets into trouble with the police, the school will usually insist that he or she is sent home. You should not try to prevent this. You will probably have to telephone the student's parents to tell them about the incident. Before you do this, discuss the phone call with any members of the staff who have previous experience of these situations. When you phone the parents stress that their child is fit and well. If you work for an agency, always keep the agency fully informed.

11.5
Coming home

When the time comes to leave the students will have mixed feelings. They will want to stay with the new friends they have found and they will also want to see their parents and old friends at home.

The procedures for the journey home will be similar to those described above except that the students will now be experienced travellers. The excessive number of small items of luggage that the students want to carry will mean that they will need to be particularly careful not to lose anything. There may also be problems with delayed or over-booked flights. If the students' arrival time is going to be delayed, they should be told to inform their parents. You may also find that it is necessary to split the group because the flight has been over-booked. If this happens you should always stay to accompany the last students to leave. It is, of course, essential that the parents are kept fully informed.

11.6
Reporting on the holiday course

When you finally hand the students over to their parents, you will probably feel relieved that your responsibilities are over. However you may be asked to write a report of the holiday course for your employer. This is easier to do if you have kept a diary during the course to support your memory. This is particularly important if there have been accidents or thefts because you may be called as a witness in legal proceedings.

When making judgements about the course, try to take a broad view of the total experience from the students' point of view. Don't be confused by unimportant details. When identifying areas in which the school has failed in its service, try to be clear and constructive. Remember that the purpose of your report is to identify both the negative and the positive aspects of the course before coming to a balanced conclusion.

As a final task, it might be a good idea for you to note down the things that you have learned through leading the group, because it has also been a learning experience for you. It will help you decide whether you want to repeat the experience in future years.

ADMINISTRATION

This section is addressed chiefly to proprietors, course directors and other administrators but contains useful background information for all who work on holiday courses or perhaps intend to start a new centre.

12

Administration

**12.0
Preparation for
the course**

Smooth and successful administration of a holiday course will result from careful preparation and planning. This planning helps to avoid crises and allows for day to day flexibility.

**12.1
Exploiting the
site**

The selection of a site and premises for a new holiday course is extremely difficult. If you want to start a new holiday course centre, you will find that most of the obvious sites in popular areas are already occupied and you will have to search for whatever is available. As far as Britain goes, you will probably still be able to find suitable premises in Wales, the Midlands and Northern England. While in Scotland, there are already a number of language schools and holiday courses in and around Edinburgh but elsewhere is still ripe for development. The same is true in Ireland with Dublin a popular centre but other places as yet underexploited. Try to avoid areas that become over-loaded with foreign students during the summer.

The site and premises will often decide the type of course which can be run. A residential private school may be suitable for children or teenagers but not for adults. Courses for very young children cannot usually take advantage of family accommodation. A course in town will offer few possibilities for rural optional activities and similarly a course in an isolated country area will find it difficult to travel to cinemas or ice skating rinks. One of the dangers of isolated schools is that they become little self-sufficient communities of foreigners and the students have no contact with local people.

The best schools exploit the potential of their position so you should investigate the local area before deciding on the type of course you will run. You may be able to offer a special 'option' in addition to the language course. Some highly successful holiday courses have offered special training in traditional sports but areas such as music, drama or the visual arts are less frequently available. In some areas you can offer more unusual outdoor activities such as sailing, rock climbing or pony trekking. Sometimes the history of the local area will suggest themes for options. I have also known of holiday courses which occupy surplus rooms in holiday camps or which have been attached to activity holidays for English-speaking children.

12.2 Recruiting staff

Just as the choice of site will influence the type of holiday course which can be run, it will also influence your selection of staff. If you have access to a private swimming pool, you will have to employ a qualified life saver. If you can use the 'arts and crafts' room, you will want to employ a teacher who can exploit it.

When recruiting staff, try to build up a team with a varied mix of skills. You will need some specialists, but you should also look for people with a range of skills and a willingness to take responsibility. A sports teacher who can also organise an excursion to a local castle is more useful than one who cannot. A language teacher might be able to lead a photography option and supervise a game of basketball. Anyone who has experience with youth clubs or other organisations for young people like the scout movement will be able to contribute very useful ideas.

Trained and qualified teachers not only know how to organise different activities but they know why they are doing them. Unqualified, inexperienced EFL or PE teachers may be able to play lots of games with the students but they have no idea whether the games have any educational value. In the context of a holiday course we recognise that participation and enjoyment are important elements and we do not insist that every activity should have a clear educational motive. However, we must recognise that a holiday course is both 'a holiday' and 'a course'.

Amongst your staff of teachers, it is very valuable to have one or two who are local to the area of the school. They will be able to make suggestions for local excursions or activities and they may have friends who could come in to speak to the students. Their knowledge of local history and geography will be very helpful.

Teachers who can speak foreign languages are very useful in emergencies with students and parents but this skill should not be regarded as essential because you will usually find another student who can help.

12.2.1 Language teachers

Although it is not essential that all the language teachers should have a specialist qualification in EFL, you will need some qualified EFL teachers who can advise and guide those who have no qualifications. Holiday courses are rarely able to pay high wages, but the teachers should always be able to see their work as a learning experience. Teachers with EFL experience are preferable to those without, but you should recognise that limited or restricted experience may negatively influence their usefulness on a holiday course. A teacher whose experience has been limited to teaching adult monolingual classes in a foreign country may try to apply the same methodology to the holiday course. This teacher might not exploit the special learning opportunities which a holiday course offers.

I remember a holiday course director who, the story goes, used to ask all prospective teachers the same question: 'Have you been to Vienna?' We used to joke that only those candidates who had been to Vienna were employed! This was, of course, an exaggeration but one can understand the principle behind the question. When employing teachers, those who have travelled widely and experienced visiting or living in a foreign language community will better understand the feelings of the holiday course students.

There are many different kinds of qualifications for EFL teachers. The RSA TEFL Certificate is usually taken after a four week intensive course. At a higher level the RSA TEFL Diploma follows a three month intensive course or a 12 month part time course. These qualifications are very useful but it should be recognised that they concentrate on the teaching of English to adults rather than children or teenagers.

Teachers who work in the American, Australian or British education system often want to do some extra work during the summer. They can be very reliable and useful staff members because they are trained in classroom management and understand how to structure learning activities. School teachers who have an element of EFL training can be ideal holiday course teachers.

You may also have applications from graduates in Linguistics or Applied Linguistics. These applicants should be treated with caution because they may be over-qualified for a holiday course and be unable to adapt their skills to young students.

12.2.2 Sports teachers

Although qualified and experienced sports teachers are preferable, students who are training to be Physical Education teachers can also be very useful on a holiday course. They have access to all the newest ideas and will be eager to try them out. Most PE students who have completed their first year of training will have the life saving certificate required by swimming teachers. Qualifications in First Aid are a great asset.

12.2.3 Welfare and administrative Staff

In these areas experience of holiday course work must be considered as more important than paper qualifications. When you are selecting staff, you will have to judge the candidate's manner and try to evaluate their potential as communicators with students, other members of staff, host families, institutions and outside contacts. They need to have a manner which communicates calm confidence and authority. They obviously need good organisational skills, financial probity and the ability to delegate.

12.2.4 Balance of the sexes

Obviously you will be looking for a balance of women and men on your staff, but if the course tends to attract more female than male students, your staff should be biased in the same way. This is particularly important with residential courses where teachers are billeted with students of the same sex.

12.2.5
Preparing the
teachers

When you interview your prospective teaching staff you will have considered the candidates' suitability for their main tasks and will have investigated the additional responsibilities (organising individual excursions or 'options') which they could undertake. Before the start of the course you will have asked them to prepare themselves for these responsibilities. Many holiday courses organise a weekend induction course for their language teachers and some also for the sports staff. These sessions are very useful, not only for explaining the administration of the course but also for the exchange of ideas amongst the staff.

Remember that the success of any course depends largely on the ability of the staff to work as a team. This may be difficult since most will meet each other for the first time at the induction course or the start of the holiday course.

In your introduction to the induction course you will probably talk about the aims of the holiday course and give some idea about how you intend to run it. Some holiday courses are rather autocratic. These may be successful commercially but they rarely encourage either staff or students to return in following years. The staff prefer to feel that their individual talents are being exploited and that their suggestions are being considered. If the staff are more fulfilled, the general atmosphere of the course is happier and this is transmitted to the students.

12.3
Administrative
structure

You may decide on some form of hierarchy and appoint supervisors or coordinators for language teaching, sports, excursions and social activities. The role of these people is to encourage and guide the other teachers. These people should not try to do all the work themselves. They should have a clear idea of what they wish to achieve for the students and should be able to transmit this idea to the rest of the staff.

Many of the sessions during the induction course will take the form of brain storming in which all the participants contribute their ideas. This type of session is very useful for revealing individual personalities and bringing out some very useful suggestions which may be used later. It is particularly useful if the induction course can take place on the premises of the holiday course because they can be a stimulus for many ideas. The sports staff need to be able to see the facilities which are available so that they can make realistic plans.

Before the induction course you should have a fairly clear idea of the budget available for each area of activity. This will also help you to decide on the suggestions which teachers make. Bear in mind that students often bring quite a lot of spending money with them and so some ideas can be proposed at an extra charge.

The induction course should lead to a draft programme for the first week's activities together with suggestions for later weeks.

**12.4
Day to day
administration
during the
course**

The most important skill for the holiday course director is delegation. The day to day work is very arduous and directors often get excessively tired. This problem is not confined to directors; it is not unknown for teachers to have breakdowns through overwork. A good director will spot the signs of this impending crisis and will insist that the teacher takes a break. Some of the younger staff may have little experience of responsibility and need assistance. This should not mean taking over the responsibility but giving suggestions and guidance. It should be seen as a learning experience for the teacher.

Remember that students enjoy taking on small responsibilities. They gain a feeling of pride from being asked to cooperate, so do not ignore this available help. Obviously, it is unfair to ask the students to do anything which is too difficult or takes up too much time.

If the period of employment of the staff is to be in excess of four weeks, you should ensure that they all have a break of a day or two away from the school during this time. You should also try to give yourself a similar break.

I may seem to have over stressed the danger of overwork but on a good holiday course, the enthusiasm for activities may well drive some staff beyond their physical limits. On a residential holiday course the days are long and maintaining enthusiasm and control with the students is very tiring. On a tightly run course, the collapse of a member of staff causes immense problems, so think in terms of prevention rather than cure.

12.4.1
Communications
with and between
teaching staff

It is difficult to organise formal meetings with all the staff because at most times of the day someone needs to be supervising the students. Group leaders should also be invited to staff meetings whenever possible. Regular meetings with groups of staff are very useful because you can discuss the success of completed activities and suggestions for new ones. Some teachers will be inhibited at large meetings so try to keep the numbers fairly small. The meetings should not take place in the staff room during a break when teachers are rushing in and out and trying to get coffee. The meeting needs to be quiet and calm. Bring notes of the things which you wish to say and take notes of any important decisions or suggestions.

Groups of teachers may also wish to meet at times when you cannot be present. This may concern the organisation of a particular event which involves that group. In this case try to get an oral report of the decisions taken.

When you want to give a message to a member of staff, try to give it verbally rather than through a written note. It is much more personal and allows the teacher a chance to protest or ask for clarification.

A noticeboard giving details of daily and future events provides a useful form of communication. It should always show which members of staff are responsible for each activity. This may be the same noticeboard which is used for the students or you can have your own board in the staff room.

12.4.2 Communications with group leaders	As I mention in the chapter for group leaders, it is most important for the school to negotiate the role of the group leaders. There is no point in complaining that they are lazy or uncooperative unless you have some agreed definition of their duties. This may be discussed directly with the group leaders or perhaps with the agency they represent.
	Group leaders should be considered as members of the staff of the school and should be encouraged to lead excursions and options, supervise sports and take part in lessons in the same way as other staff members. You will not be able to expect as much of the group leaders as you will of the others but they should be expected to make their contribution. You may wish to meet with group leaders separately or together with other members of staff. This decision will probably depend on the topic to be discussed.
12.4.3 Communications with students	Some schools have regular morning assemblies at which the events of the day are explained and notice is given of future events. These are very good for developing a sense of cohesion and unity amongst the students but it is difficult to address a large group in language which is understandable to all. When large groups are together it is difficult to be sure that you have the attention of all the students. The same problems occur if notices are given at communal meals.
	Language teachers find members of staff giving notices during their lessons rather annoying because it seems to break up the flow of work. These teachers should understand the importance of this means of communication. Another person brings a different voice to the classroom which is always good. The teacher can use the notices as a listening comprehension exercise for the students by asking them to take notes and then produce an oral summary. The notices can also lead to discussion.

Contents of School Orientation Pack

Letter of welcome from course director

Personal student identity card

List of school rules (including host family rules where necessary)

Street map of local area showing school, post office, banks, etc.

Names of staff giving responsibilities, illustrated with photographs

Plan of school premises

Class timetable

The disturbance caused by the interruptions can be reduced by warning the teachers of the time when they are to take place so that the teachers can plan their lessons accordingly. With lower level classes, the teacher can also spend some valuable time by taking the class to look at the school notice board so that they can read and talk about the notices.

A course director may well provide set times when students can come and talk about their problems but you will probably find that you will learn more through less formal contacts with the students during meals or while dealing with the school bank. The teachers and group leaders will be your most useful sources of information.

12.4.4 Communications between staff and students

Even in a small school the major difficulty with communication is identification. Some schools insist that students wear name badges at least for the first few days. I know of one school where all the teachers wear red sweat shirts (provided by the school) so that they can be identified at a distance. It is a good idea for all members of staff to wear clearly legible name badges (perhaps in a different colour from the students). On or near the noticeboard you can put up a display of photographs of yourself and the staff (including group leaders), clearly labelled with their names. You will find this invaluable when you are asking a student 'Who told you to come here?' and he or she replies 'I don't know, one of the teachers.'

Try to discourage the staff from using foreign languages when communicating with the students. It may start as a game but develop in a way which will ruin the purpose of the holiday course. It also leads to distinctions between students. The staff may include speakers of the main European languages but if these languages are used the Turkish, Finnish, Arab, Japanese, Israeli or Iranian students will all feel marginalised.

The staff should speak English to the students and expect the students to reply in the same language at all times. Teachers of all subjects need to learn the technique of speaking clearly and patience in waiting for the reply. The group leaders should be encouraged to follow the same practice most of the time. It would be cruel to try to ban the students talking to each other in their native language. It is hard for some of us to understand quite how exhausting it is to be surrounded by a little known foreign language for hours on end. This being said, we should try to organise activities in ways which will encourage the use of English.

12.5 Health and safety

The director of a course is ultimately responsible for the health and safety of the students and staff. Safety procedures need not be inconvenient or uninteresting. A fire practice held at midnight can be an exciting adventure for the students.

12.5.1 Fire safety

The premises which you use for the school should have been inspected and passed as safe by the local fire department. If you put students into premises which have not been passed, you may well be breaking the law. Local fire departments often insist on the installation of safety measures such as extinguishers, fire doors or emergency escapes. You should ensure that fire doors are kept shut and that access to emergency escapes is not blocked. The British Council in their handbook on the Recognition of

Language Schools, insist that all rooms (including classrooms) should display clear fire safety instructions. Once again, this should not be seen as an annoying chore, but as the stimulus for a useful language lesson.

Students should be made aware of the dangers of fire both in the school and when walking in the country. Cigarettes are a frequent cause of fire and so smoking should not be allowed in classrooms or bedrooms.

12.5.2 Health

A local doctor should be responsible for dealing with accidents and illnesses occurring amongst the staff or students. Even though you will probably have a member of staff who is qualified in first aid, you should always refer any problem, except the most trivial, to the local doctor. Some schools operate a consultation service for students who are unwell but if you do this never give any medicines (including aspirin) to the students. Your students' enrolment forms should give you details of health problems but do not assume that if none are listed then none exist.

Food poisoning is not uncommon. This may sound rather dramatic but it may take many forms. The most serious would be the mass poisoning of staff and students through school meals. This is unlikely because professional caterers are scrupulous about hygiene. More frequent are minor attacks caused by students eating food which they have stored in cupboards or other unsuitable places. They should also be warned about buying hamburgers from street stalls.

As has been mentioned earlier, in the chapter on sports, when accidents occur always get properly qualified help. Make sure that the student's parents (and the study tours agency if there is one) are informed and that a written report is prepared. The school should have an insurance policy to cover accident liability and you would be well advised to acquaint yourself with its provisions!

12.5.3 Road safety

In most English-speaking countries except the United States and Canada you drive on the left. Many students will be unaccustomed to this, which means that they are in constant danger when crossing roads. However, cars do stop at pedestrian crossings in Britain and so students should be expected to use them. They should be taught how to use the pedestrian operated traffic lights at some crossings.

At some centres, students often hire bicycles. This presents extra hazards as although they may be competent cyclists, they are not accustomed to local ways of driving. Course directors will have to decide on means of training students in bicycle safety before allowing them to hire bicycles. The local police may be prepared to help in this task.

Some schools transport students in cars or minibuses which are driven by members of staff. (Have you checked that your insurance policy allows this?) At these times, and whenever the students are travelling by road transport they should be instructed always to get out on the correct side of the vehicle.

Before you drive a school vehicle

1 Have you got a valid driving licence for this vehicle?

2 Are you in a fit state to drive?

3 Are you and your passengers fully insured?

4 Where is the insurance certificate?

5 Do you know the way to your destination and back to the school?

6 Do you know the school's emergency phone number?

7 Do you have suitable money for making a phone call?

8 Is the vehicle covered by an emergency breakdown service, if so what is the phone number?

9 Are there enough seats for the passengers?

10 Are there seat belts? Do the passengers know how to belt up AND release the belts!

11 Have you got all the necessary documents in case of accident or breakdown?

12 Is the vehicle in a roadworthy condition?

13 Is there sufficient fuel, oil and water?

14 Does the vehicle use diesel fuel, leaded or unleaded petrol?

15 Have you got enough cash to cover emergencies?

16 Have you driven this vehicle before?

17 Are you familiar with all controls including lights and windscreen wipers?

18 Is this vehicle subject to special speed restrictions?

19 Does the Course Director know when you should arrive back?

20 In the event of your death or incapacity due to an accident, have you got documents which identify you and give the address and phone number of the school?

**12.6
Passports,
identity cards,
air tickets and
money**

Many schools prefer to take these items for safe keeping when the young students arrive at the school. The school then operates a daily 'school bank' so that students can ask for small sums as they need them. The money and other documents should be kept in a safe because often the total value will be quite considerable. Students will sometimes need their passport or national identity card in order to change traveller's cheques or foreign money.

Most schools give the students some form of identification for use if they get lost. This should contain their name, nationality, the school address and phone number and the name, address and phone number of the host family (if they have one). The school telephone should be manned at all times to deal with any emergencies.

School Identity card

COSHAM SCHOOL OF ENGLISH

361, Victory Road, Cosham, PO3 3TH   0705-144361

NAME Stefania Rossi   AGE 17

NATIONALITY Italian

HOST FAMILY Mrs Rogers, 17, Connaught Lane, Cosham 0705 134429

ARRIVAL DATE 12-6-89

DEPARTURE DATE 25-6-89

IN EMERGENCY PLEASE CONTACT THE SCHOOL

Theft of a student's money or property often spoils an otherwise enjoyable holiday course. Nothing you can do will totally eradicate these unfortunate incidents but you can take some measures to reduce their likelihood. Students on holiday courses often bring more money than they have ever seen before. As far as possible try to prevent students from holding large sums in cash. Most students do not bring jewellery but they will probably have cameras, cassette players and other expensive items. If possible these should be kept secure in individual lockers or failing this in cupboards in bedrooms.

12.7
Controlling your budget

Holiday courses are usually run on a fairly tight budget. Successful administration is often the result of careful budget planning. Controlling your budget is not easy because you rarely know the exact number of students in the school until the very last moment. When you are planning the budget for optional excursions, the cost will vary according to the number of students who opt for the trip. The difference in cost between a 48 seat coach and a 56 seat coach is minimal. When offering an option you will need to state the minimum participation which will allow you to cover your expenses.

If you are going to delegate the planning of options and excursions, you will need to give the teachers a clear idea of the money which they can spend. Once again, this is a valuable learning task for the teachers.

12.7.1
Inclusive or extra?

Many schools pride themselves that the basic charge for the course is all-inclusive and students will not need to pay for any optional activities. This is fine for the students but it makes it very difficult to budget for a flexible programme which reflects the students' interests. This variety is easier to offer if the students pay extra fees for each excursion or optional activity in which they participate. In this way each activity can be separately budgeted.

If the school offers all-inclusive fees you will have to calculate the amount of the fee which is available for options and excursions. Remember that a sum is also necessary for day to day expenses of the school. If a tennis tournament is to lead to prizes, you will have to put aside money to pay for those prizes. If you are going to offer arts and crafts 'options' you will need money for materials. If you are going to offer a video in the evening, you will need money to hire it.

12.7.2
Making money

Schools which charge for optional excursions and activity can budget to make a small profit on these so that they can appear to be more generous in other ways. In all-inclusive schools, you can make a little money by running a shop selling sweets, snacks and soft drinks. Some schools have T-shirts or sweat shirts printed with the school name and logo and these are also sold to the students at a profit.

The students will probably take a lot of photographs during the period of the holiday course. The school, in collaboration with a local photographic shop, could easily offer a service which would allow the students to hand their exposed films to the school shop and later collect their prints and negatives. This service would encourage the taking of photographs and could also make a little money.

Some schools ask a local photographer or one of the staff to take group photographs of the classes or sports teams. The school can make a small profit by selling these to the students.

12.8
The telephone

Telephone calls from parents to their children can be the biggest annoyance in the life of teachers and administrators on residential holiday courses. On a large site, it is often very difficult to find the students to receive the calls and you can spend hours running all over the school trying to trace a student. It also means that staff have to be on a rota to take charge of the phone. This is less of a problem when students are in family accommodation because they will probably receive calls with the family. You should tell the students that they may not make phone calls from their host family telephone unless they ask permission and pay for the call.

12.8.1
Phone cards

Given sufficient time, the Telecom service is usually able to put in an extra line for outgoing calls which uses magnetic phone cards to pay for the calls. Many residential schools have found that this can be at least a partial solution to the telephone problems. Students buy phone cards from the school and use them to call home. This greatly reduces the cost of calls because the parents do not have to hold on for expensive minutes whilst the student is being found.

12.8.2
Telephone
appointments

An alternative solution is for the students to have appointments for receiving calls from their parents. When making notes of these appointments, it is important that parents are reminded of the time difference there may be. Appointments can lead to large groups of noisy students gathering around the office during the hours when the calls are expected. They often wander away because of boredom and the duty teacher has to send someone to find the student.

12.8.3
The psychological
effect of
telephone calls

Students who are homesick are often more tearful after a phone call than before. After the first two or three days, most students find the calls from their parents rather a nuisance. They have begun to enjoy the freedom of being away from their parents and the calls tend to interrupt them when they are with their friends.

Although we tend to notice the effect of calls on students, we should also think of the parents. Every parent should be contacted on the first evening so that they can be reassured that the journey was safe. If you are operating a phone card system many students will become so involved in the holiday course that they will forget to phone their parents. The parents will be sitting at home in an unusually quiet house and worrying about what their child is doing. You will still receive calls from parents asking their children to phone. In this case don't simply pass on the message, make sure that the student does make a call.

12.9
Discipline

The holiday course director is usually the ultimate authority for discipline. Remember that any large group of young students is likely to cause some discipline problems. When that group is made up of teenagers with many different cultural backgrounds who have been released from the controlling influence of their parents, you should not be shocked by some misbehaviour. The students are in a new situation and they don't know the rules.

One potential source of bad behaviour is tension between national or racial groups. This is particularly damaging and every effort should be made to avoid this before it starts. As has been mentioned earlier, you should try to avoid organising the students in national groups for any activities (with the possible exception of the International Evening performances). Students should be encouraged to feel a loyalty which does not relate to nationality. In some cases, a 'house' system, in which all the students are divided into international teams can help to develop this non-national loyalty. If a student is a member and supporter of the Blue Team, he or she is less likely to feel that he is one of the French aganist the Spanish.

The second potential source of bad behaviour is directed towards the local community. We all know how insular and prejudiced the British (and other host communities) can be. Both in large towns like Brighton or Bournemouth and in small villages, the influx of a large number of foreign students causes tension. If the students hang around the streets in large groups, making noise and dropping litter, they will be condemned as a group of foreigners rather than as a group of young people. The school needs the support and goodwill of the local community and so you should try to avoid alienating them.

There is also an element of tension between the local youth and the foreign students. If the locals feel that their hamburger bars or amusement arcades have been 'invaded' by foreigners, they are likely to display their resentment. This can be made worse by the superficial affluence of the foreign students. There is little that can be done about this problem except to avoid it. There should be no reason for groups of your students to hang about the streets in the evenings if your programme of social and cultural activities is well organised.

12.9.1 Code of behaviour

It is very difficult for students to behave well if they don't know what behaviour is expected of them. If we have fairly clear expectations of student behaviour we should explain these to students. Some schools have prepared small booklets (in the same style as those produced for host families) in which they explain administrative things about the school and outline the rules of behaviour. This does not seem excessively authoritarian if you take the trouble to explain why each restriction is imposed.

The rules will include norms of dress, attitudes to punctuality, politeness, laws about smoking and drinking, warnings about drugs and explicit sexual behaviour and so on. The booklet should not be simply a list of negatives but should give guidance on what is acceptable behaviour. 'Fitting In', published by Language Teaching Publications, is well worth using in this respect. The material should not simply be given to the students, it should be used as the basis for language lessons in the first few days of the course.

12.9.2 Sanctions

The school always reserves the right to send home a student who has seriously misbehaved. Before using this ultimate sanction, try to consider the student's behaviour in a reasonable perspective. Recognise that the need to send the student home is an indication of your own failure as much as it is a condemnation of the student. Be sure to examine your own procedures and attitudes to see if you could prevent the repetition of this situation.

12.10 Quality control

The director of a holiday language course needs to establish high standards and to make sure that those standards are maintained and so procedures for quality control are an essential part of any administration.

Quality control can be divided into two parts: customer satisfaction and maintenance of standards. Customer satisfaction cannot be measured by simply greeting students in the corridor and saying 'Things going all right then?' and assuming that a positive reply is an indication of a satisfied customer. If you really care about what the customers think you must make a serious attempt to learn their views. A questionnaire is a good way of doing this, particularly if the responses are written in the students' native languages. Those of us who have tried to complain about a meal or hotel accommodation whilst abroad will know the hindrance of limited command of the language.

Quality Control Letter

Checks on customer satisfaction need not only occur at the end of a course. It would not be difficult to organise spot checks after a lesson, an excursion, sporting activity or social event. The advantage of these spot checks is that they will give you time to make immediate improvements. The information in the leaving letter only benefits students in later courses.

Another useful source of information is the staff and group leaders. If they are dedicated professionals they will be quick to spot opportunities for improved standards. Unless the director creates a channel for communicating these ideas (and a procedure for recording them), they will float away like all staff room chatter.

The holiday course brochure will describe the standards which you claim to offer. All too often these brochures are written months before the course takes place and the text has been forgotten by the time the course starts. It would be a useful exercise to look back at the text of your brochure after the beginning of the course to check whether those standards are being maintained.

To a large degree the course director will probably delegate responsibility for quality control to the DOS, Sports Director and others, but you should also check that this work is being done properly by visiting classes, attending sports events, eating meals, checking dormitories and so on.

When things go wrong you should be less concerned with apportioning blame than investigating whether any failure of procedures contributed to the incident. Of course your first duty will be to solve the immediate problem but this should lead to a review of procedures which will be beneficial for all concerned.

COSHAM SCHOOL OF ENGLISH

Dear . . . .

We hope that you have had a happy and useful holiday course with us at the Cosham School of English. It would be useful for us if you could tell us your feelings about your course and about any improvements we could make.

What did you think of:

The English Lessons	**Good**	**OK**	**Bad**
The Accommodation	**Good**	**OK**	**Bad**
The Food	**Good**	**OK**	**Bad**
The Social Activities	**Good**	**OK**	**Bad**
The Sports	**Good**	**OK**	**Bad**
The Excursions	**Good**	**OK**	**Bad**

Would you like to come to this school again?   **Yes**   **No**

Was there anything which you particularly enjoyed on the course? Was there anything you didn't like? Write in English or your own language.

. . . .
. . . .
. . . .
. . . .
. . . .

Thank you very much for your help,

Anne Richards

Course Director

12.11
Conclusions

The aims of a holiday course are usually expressed strictly in terms of language development. The actual benefit to students is much broader. Students return from a successful holiday course as much more mature and independent individuals. Their outlook on life has broadened. Their attitudes to foreigners are more informed. They are more skilled at handling relationships with adults and people of their own age.

Many of these benefits may not be seen immediately but will appear in the long term. Unless those who work on holiday courses recognise these facts, they cannot be expected to provide opportunities for this development to take place.